ENROLLED AGENT EXAM PREP PLUS

1000+ REVIEW QUESTIONS

FOR THE IRS SPECIAL ENROLLMENT EXAMINATION

PART 1, PART 2 AND PART 3

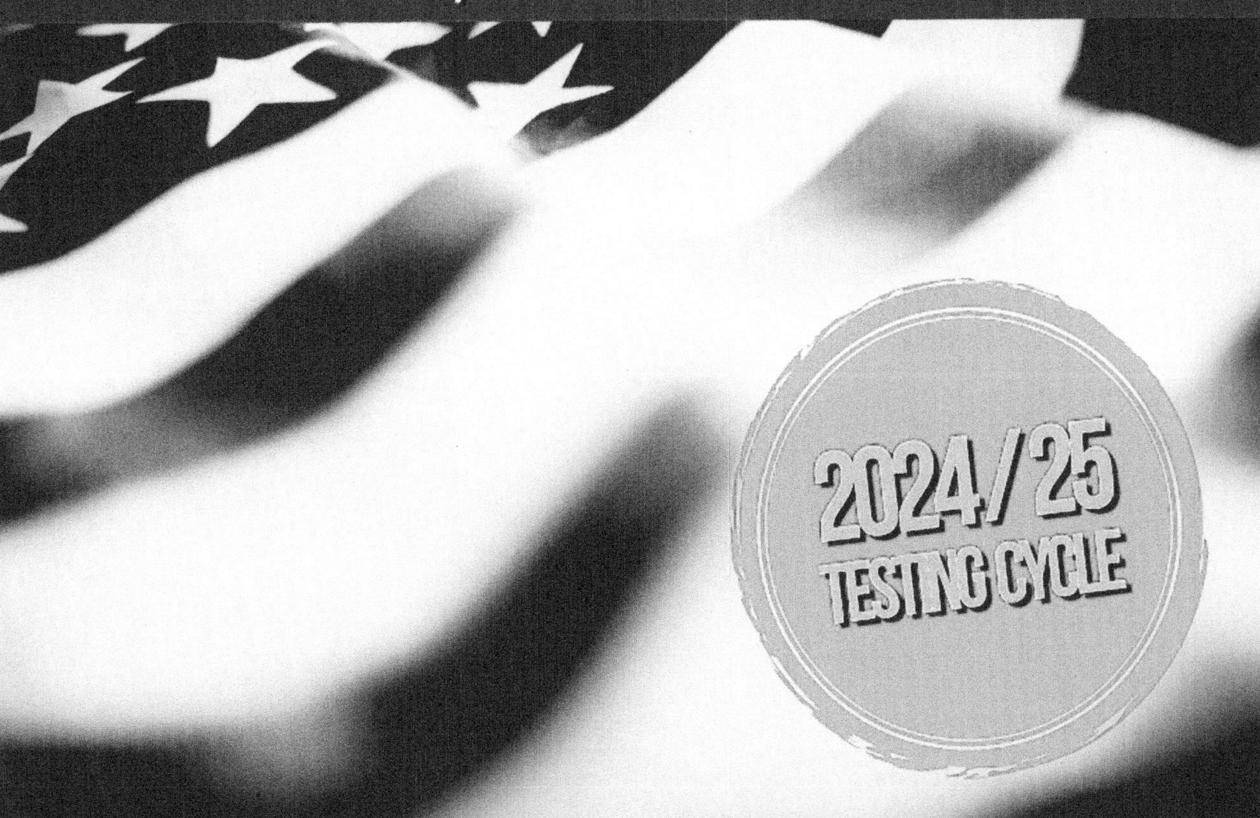

SKILLPREP BOOKS

Welcome to *SkillPrep Books!*

As a thank-you gift for choosing us, **this book includes free additional content. You can GET IT HERE:**

FREE ADDITIONAL CONTENT

For any inquiries, suggestions, or assistance, feel free to email me directly at: ***kennydodgers@skillprepbooks.com***

Warm regards,

Kenneth Dodgers
founder of SkillPrep Books

Last revision: July 26, 2024

Table of Contents (1/2)

Table of Contents (2/2)

What Does the EA Exam Cover?

The exam is presented in three different sections:
Part 1: Individuals
Part 2: Businesses
Part 3: Representation

Each examination consists of 100 questions. But only 85 of your answers count.
The rest of the questions are for quantitative analysis purposes.
You'll never know which ones those are.

Each part is **3.5 hours long**. The actual seat time is 4 hours to allow for a tutorial, survey, and one scheduled 15-minute break. The examination parts can be taken in any order.

Each exam part may be taken 4 times per testing window, which runs **from May 1, 2024 to February 28, 2025**. The test is not offered during the annual blackout period in March and April. During this time the test is updated for the most recent tax law. You have a total of two years from the time you pass your first exam to pass all three parts and become an Enrolled Agent.

The parts of the examination are:

1 - Individuals
This section deals with the individual taxpayer and includes many topics and forms, broken down into these 6 areas:

- Section 1: Preliminary Work and Taxpayer Data *(14 questions)*
- Section 2: Income and Assets *(17 questions)*
- Section 3: Deductions and Credits *(17 questions)*
- Section 4: Taxation and Advice *(15 questions)*
- Section 5: Advising the Individual Taxpayer *(11 questions)*
- Section 6: Specialized Returns for Individuals *(11 questions)*

2 - Businesses

Many tax professionals work with individuals and their personal tax returns. To make a living in today's tax environment, you must grow your practice by taking on business clients.

This is where your day-to-day income will come from – through accounting, consulting, safeguarding the client's business from employee theft, and helping them do tax planning. You can become indispensable to a business by knowing the relevant loopholes.

The Part 2 exam covers these topics:

- Section 1: Businesses *(30 questions)*
- Section 2: Business Financial Information *(37 questions)*
- Section 3: Specialized Returns and Taxpayers *(18 questions)*

3 - Representation, Practices and Procedures

This is the fun stuff, and is what makes you stand apart as an Enrolled Agent. This is what distinguishes you from the run-of-the-mill tax return preparer – and even from CPAs. To prepare your client's case for Tax Court (even though you may not practice there, yourself), you must learn several topics broken down into the following 4 areas:

- Section 1: Practices and Procedures *(26 questions)*
- Section 2: Representation before the IRS *(25 questions)*
- Section 3: Specific Types of Representation *(20 questions)*
- Section 4: Completion of the Filing Process *(14 questions)*

The examinations are closed books, so no reference materials, papers, or study materials are allowed at the test center. You will not be able to leave the testing room with a copy of any notes taken during the examination. Some examination questions may contain excerpts from the Internal Revenue Code or Income Tax Regulations.

You can schedule an examination appointment at any time online at ***www.prometric.com/test-takers/search/irs***

or by calling 800-306-3926 between 8 a.m. and 9 p.m. (ET), Monday through Friday.

You will receive a number confirming your appointment. Keep this confirmation number for your records - you will need it to reschedule, cancel, or change your appointment.
You may take each part of the examination at your convenience and in any order.
Parts do not have to be taken on the same day or on consecutive days.

A confirmation email is sent containing the date time and location of the exam. If any information on the confirmation notice is incorrect, if you have not received your confirmation notice before your exam date, or if you lose your confirmation email, you can log back into your dashboard and request a duplicate confirmation.
Keep in mind that you are not allowed to take anything into the room, including jewelry, purse, wallet, or watch. A locked locker is available for your personal effects, and you must turn all of your pockets inside out for security.
The test center provides you with scratch paper, 2 pencils, and a handheld calculator. You will also be able to use an on-screen calculator during the examination.
After completing the exam, you press the "End" button. You will be asked about 5-10 evaluation questions. When you press "End" the second time, the results come up on your screen. If you pass, the score report will show a passing designation. It will not show a score. All score values above passing indicate that a candidate is qualified.

You will also receive diagnostic information, which will indicate areas where you may wish to consider professional development. When you pass all three parts of the examination, you may apply for enrollment with the IRS.

If you fail, your score report will show a scaled score between 40 and 104. You will also receive diagnostic information to assist you with future examination preparation. Diagnostic information will show an indicator of 1, 2, or 3, meaning:

Area of weakness: Additional study is necessary.

You need to focus on this area as you prepare to take the test again.

You may want to consider taking a course or participating actively in a study group on this topic.

Marginal: You may need additional study in this area.

Strong: You clearly demonstrated an understanding of this subject area.

This information is designed to help you prepare for retaking the examination.

You may take each part of the examination at your convenience and in any order. Examination parts do not have to be taken on the same day or on consecutive days. You may take examination parts up to four times each during each test window. If you fail any part of the examination, you must allow a 24-hour waiting period before rescheduling a retest.

You must reschedule with Prometric online at ***www.prometric.com/test-takers/search/irs or by calling 800-306-3926.***

If you do not pass a part of the examination after four attempts during the May 1 to February 28 test window, you must wait until the next test window before attempting to retake any failed part of the examination again. The average passing rate for Part 1 of the exam in 2022 was about 80%. For Part 2, the average passing rate was about 60%, and for Part 3, the average passing rate was about 85%. For this reason, we recommend that candidates attempt Part 1 first followed by Part 3 and then Part 2. We also strongly recommend extra time in your preparation for Part 2.

When you pass all three parts of the examination, you need to file
Form 23 - Application for Enrollment to Practice Before the Internal Revenue Service.
As part of the evaluation of your enrollment application, the Internal Revenue Service will conduct a suitability check that will include a review of your personal tax compliance.

This book was developed to assist readers in IRS Enrolled Agent exam preparation. It has gone through multiple review cycles to produce a high-quality text. However, there are no representations or warranties, express or implied, about the completeness, accuracy, reliability, suitability, or availability concerning the information, products, or related graphics contained in this book for any purpose. All references are provided as indications only. The information presented is meant for learning purposes. The author does not accept any legal responsibility for the content within. By using this book, the reader agrees to indemnify and hold harmless the author and publisher from any damages claimed because of the content of this book.

IRS® is a registered trademark and did not partake in the development of this publication. IRS does not endorse or otherwise sponsor this publication and makes no warranty, guarantee, or representation, express or implied, as to its accuracy or content.

Book Structure and Content

This book comprises a comprehensive collection of exercises designed to enhance and test your knowledge.

It includes **615 multiple-choice questions**, allowing readers to select the correct option from a set of answers. Additionally, there are **355 fill-in-the-blank questions/statements**, challenging you to recall and enter the correct word or phrase. For those seeking to further demonstrate their understanding, the book also features **40 open-ended questions**, providing an opportunity for more detailed responses.
Overall, with **over 1,000 questions**, this book offers a thorough examination of the subject matter.

NOTE: The questions were designed to encompass a broad spectrum of the tax code and IRS procedures relevant to individual taxpayers, including specific scenarios, forms, and regulations. While some forms or topics might appear in multiple questions, the intent was to highlight different aspects or uses to ensure a well-rounded understanding of their application in various tax situations.

PART 1

INDIVIDUALS

Multiple-Choice Questions

Part I - Section 1: Preliminary Work and Taxpayer Data

1.What tax form is used to report income earned from freelance work or contract work?

a) Form W-2 b) Form 1040 c) Form 1099-NEC d) Form 1099-R

2.Which document is used to report income earned from interest on a savings account?

a) Form W-2 b) Form 1099-INT c) Form 1040 d) Form 1099-MISC

3.When might a taxpayer use Form W-4?

a) To report self-employment income

b) To calculate Social Security tax

c) To calculate federal income tax withholding from employee paychecks

d) To determine the amount of Medicare tax owed

4.Which taxpayer identification number is generally used by non-resident aliens who don't have a Social Security Number?

a) Social Security Number (SSN)

b) Employer Identification Number (EIN)

c) Individual Taxpayer Identification Number (ITIN)

d) Adoption Taxpayer Identification Number (ATIN)

5.Under what circumstance might a taxpayer file Form 9465, Installment Agreement Request?

a) To request an extension of time to file taxes

b) To report income from a partnership c) To report income from rental property

d) To request a payment plan for tax liabilities they can't pay in full

6.What is the primary purpose of Form W-9?

a) To report income from investments

b) To calculate Medicare tax

c) To request a taxpayer's identification number for information reporting purposes

d) To determine the amount of federal income tax owed

7.A taxpayer can use Form 8822 for which of the following reasons?

a) To request a copy of a tax return

b) To change their address with the IRS

c) To file an amended tax return

d) To report income from self-employment

8.When might a taxpayer use Form 8822, Change of Address?

a) When they change their email address

b) When they move to a new city

c) When they change their phone number

d) When they change their last name due to marriage

9.What is the primary purpose of Form 4868, Application for Automatic Extension of Time to File U.S. Individual Income Tax Return?

a) To request an extension of time to file taxes

b) To claim a refund or correct errors on a previously filed tax return

c) To report income from rental property

d) To request a payment plan for tax liabilities

10.Which form should an individual use to report income earned from a dividend?

a) Form W-2 b) Form 1040 c) Form 1099-DIV d) Form 1099-R

11. What is the standard deduction amount for a single filer in 2024?

a) $14,200 b) $14,600 c) $14,550 d) $14,800

12.What is the primary purpose of Form 1095-C, Employer-Provided Health Insurance Offer and Coverage?

a) To report income from investments

b) To report changes in income to the IRS

c) To report health insurance coverage information provided by an employer

d) To claim a tax credit for education expenses

13. Which of the following taxpayers is required to file a tax return?

a) A single person under 65 with a gross income of $10,300

b) A single person over 65 with a gross income of $11,700

c) A married couple filing jointly, both under 65, with a gross income of $20,400

d) A married couple filing jointly, one spouse 65 or older, with a gross income of $24,800

14. When might a taxpayer use Form 8821, Tax Information Authorization?

a) To report income from a partnership

b) To request an extension of time to file taxes

c) To authorize a representative to receive tax information

d) To claim a tax credit for child and dependent care expenses

15. What is the primary purpose of Form 1098, Mortgage Interest Statement?

a) To report income from rental property b) To report income from freelance work

c) To report mortgage interest received or paid d) To report income from investments

16. Which of the following is not a purpose of Form W-4?

a) To determine the employee's tax withholding amount

b) To update personal information for employer records

c) To report independent contractor income

d) To claim allowances or exemptions

17. When might a taxpayer use Form 14157, Complaint: Tax Return Preparer?

a) To report income from investments

b) To file a complaint against a tax return preparer

c) To request an extension of time to file taxes

d) To report income from rental property

18. What is the primary purpose of Form 4506, Request for Copy of Tax Return?

a) To request an extension of time to file taxes

b) To report changes in income to the IRS

c) To request a copy of a previously filed tax return

d) To authorize a representative to receive tax information

19. Which of the following statements about filing status is true?

a) Taxpayers who are legally separated under a divorce decree can file as Married Filing Jointly.

b) Married taxpayers living apart can never file as Head of Household.

c) Widows with dependent children can file as Qualifying Widow(er) for two years following the year of their spouse's death.

d) Single filers include individuals who are divorced or legally separated according to state law at the end of the year.

20. When might a taxpayer use Form 433-D, Installment Agreement?

a) To report income from freelance work b) To request an extension of time to file taxes c) To set up a payment plan for tax liabilities d) To report income from a partnership

21. When might a taxpayer use Form 1099-DIV?

a) To report income from freelance work b) To report dividend income from investments c) To report rental income d) To report income from a partnership

22. What is the primary purpose of Form 1098-E, Student Loan Interest Statement?

a) To report income from freelance work b) To report interest paid on student loans

c) To report rental income d) To report income from investments

23. Which taxpayer identification number is used by a U.S. citizen or resident alien?

a) Employer Identification Number (EIN)

b) Individual Taxpayer Identification Number (ITIN)

c) Social Security Number (SSN)

d) Adoption Taxpayer Identification Number (ATIN)

24. When might a taxpayer use Form 8938, Statement of Specified Foreign Financial Assets?

a) To report income from rental property

b) To report changes in income to the IRS

c) To report foreign financial assets

d) To report income from freelance work

25. The American Opportunity Tax Credit is available for which of the following?

a) Graduate students in their first year

b) Undergraduates for the first four years of post-secondary education

c) Students pursuing a certificate program

d) Non-resident aliens

26.Which document is used to report income from a state tax refund?

a) Form W-2 b) Form 1099-G c) Form 1040 d) Form 1099-NEC

27.When might a taxpayer use Form 8027, Employer's Annual Information Return of Tip Income and Allocated Tips?

a) To report income from a partnership b) To report tip income and allocated tips

c) To report changes in income to the IRS d) To report income from freelance work

28.What is the primary purpose of Form 1099-OID, Original Issue Discount?

a) To report income from investments b) To report changes in income to the IRS

c) To report income from rental property d) To report income from a partnership

29. Which form is used by an individual to report income from self-employment?

a) Form 1040 b) Schedule C c) Schedule SE d) Form W-2

30. When might a taxpayer use Form 1040-X, Amended U.S. Individual Income Tax Return?

a) To request an extension of time to file taxes b) To report income from freelance work

c) To correct errors on a previously filed tax return d) To report income from rental property

31.What is the primary purpose of Form 1099-K, Payment Card and Third-Party Network Transactions?

a) To report income from freelance work

b) To report interest income

c) To report income received through payment card or third-party network transactions

d) To report rental income

32. Which of the following is a correct statement about dependency exemptions?

a) A taxpayer can claim a dependency exemption for a friend who has lived with them all year.

b) Dependency exemptions are allowed for taxpayers and their spouses.

c) Dependency exemptions are phased out at high-income levels.

d) Every taxpayer is allowed one personal exemption and one for each dependent.

33. When is the deadline for filing individual tax returns (Form 1040) for the year 2024?

a) April 15, 2024 b) May 17, 2024 c) June 15, 2024 d) July 15, 2024

34. What is the primary purpose of Form 8962, Premium Tax Credit (PTC)?

a) To report income from freelance work

b) To claim a tax credit for health coverage premiums

c) To report rental income d) To report changes in income to the IRS

35. Which of the following is considered taxable income?

a) Child support payments received

b) Life insurance proceeds received due to the death of the insured person

c) Unemployment compensation

d) Gifts and inheritances

36. For which of the following situations would a taxpayer not be eligible for the Earned Income Tax Credit (EITC)?

a) They have investment income exceeding $3,650

b) They are filing as Married Filing Separately

c) They have three qualifying children

d) They earned income from working abroad

37. What is the primary purpose of Form 5498, IRA Contributions Information?

a) To report income from investments

b) To report changes in income to the IRS

c) To report IRA contributions made during the tax year

d) To report income from rental property

38.When might a taxpayer use Form 709, United States Gift (and Generation-Skipping Transfer) Tax Return?

a) To report income from freelance work

b) To report changes in income to the IRS

c) To report gifts exceeding the annual exclusion amount

d) To report income from a partnership

39. A dependent must meet certain tests to qualify for the dependency exemption. Which of the following is not one of those tests?

a) The Gross Income Test

b) The Support Test

c) The Age Test

d) The Joint Return Test

40.What is the primary purpose of Form 8965, Health Coverage Exemptions?

a) To claim a tax credit for health coverage premiums

b) To report income from investments

c) To report rental income

d) To claim an exemption from the requirement to have health coverage

Part I - Section 2: Income and Assets

1. Royalties received from oil, gas, or mineral properties are taxed as:
a) Self-employment income b) Investment income c) Ordinary income d) Capital gains

2. When might a taxpayer use Schedule C (Form 1040), Profit or Loss from Business?
a) To report income from investments
b) To report income from rental property
c) To report income from self-employment or a sole proprietorship
d) To report income from a partnership

3. Interest income from which of the following sources is typically exempt from federal income tax?
a) Corporate bonds
b) Certificates of Deposit (CDs)
c) U.S. Treasury bonds
d) Money Market Accounts

4. What is the primary purpose of Form 4797, Sales of Business Property?
a) To report income from investments b) To report income from a partnership
c) To report gains or losses from the sale of business property d) To report rental income

5. When might a taxpayer use Form 1099-B, Proceeds from Broker and Barter Exchange Transactions?
a) To report income from a partnership
b) To report income from rental property
c) To report gains or losses from securities transactions
d) To report income from freelance work

6. Which form is used to report sales and other dispositions of capital assets?
a) Form 1099-B b) Schedule D
c) Form 4797 d) Form 6252

7.When might a taxpayer use Form 8949, Sales and Other Dispositions of Capital Assets?

a) To report income from investments

b) To report income from rental property

c) To report gains or losses from the sale of stocks, bonds, or real estate

d) To report income from a partnership

8.What is the primary purpose of Form 6252, Installment Sale Income?

a) To report income from investments

b) To report gains from the sale of property where the seller receives payments over time

c) To report income from a partnership

d) To report income from rental property

9.Which tax form is used to report income earned from royalties?

a) Form 1099-R b) Form 1040 c) Form 1099-MISC d) Form 1099-INT

10.When might a taxpayer use Form 8283, Noncash Charitable Contributions?

a) To report income from investments b) To report noncash donations exceeding $500

c) To report income from rental property d) To report income from a partnership

11.Which form is used to report income from rental real estate, royalties, partnerships, S corporations, estates, trusts, and residual interests in REMICs?

a) Form W-2 b) Form 1099-MISC c) Form 1099-INT d) Schedule E (Form 1040)

12.What is the primary purpose of Form 8824, Like-Kind Exchanges?

a) To report income from investments

b) To report gains or losses from the exchange of property

c) To report income from a partnership

d) To report income from rental property

13.When might a taxpayer use Form 1099-C, Cancellation of Debt?

a) To report income from a partnership b) To report cancellation of debt exceeding $600

c) To report income from investments d) To report income from rental property

14. Which tax form is used to report income from self-employment, including freelance work or independent contracting?

a) Form 1040 b) Form W-2 c) Schedule C (Form 1040) d) Form 1099-MISC

15. When might a taxpayer use Form 3921, Exercise of an Incentive Stock Option Under Section 422(b)?

a) To report income from investments

b) To report the exercise of incentive stock options

c) To report income from a partnership

d) To report income from rental property

16. Alimony received under a divorce decree finalized after December 31, 2018, is:

a) Taxable to the recipient

b) Deductible by the payer

c) Not taxable to the recipient and not deductible by the payer

d) Reported on Form 1040, Line 2a

17. What is the term for the period over which an asset is depreciated?

a) Depreciation span b) Useful life c) Asset lifecycle d) Recovery period

18. What is the primary purpose of Form 8938, Statement of Specified Foreign Financial Assets?

a) To report income from investments

b) To report gains or losses from the sale of property

c) To report specified foreign financial assets

d) To report income from rental property

19. For tax purposes, which of the following is considered a capital asset?

a) Inventory

b) Accounts receivable

c) Personal car

d) Supplies

20.When might a taxpayer use Form 1099-S, Proceeds from Real Estate Transactions?

a) To report income from rental property

b) To report income from investments

c) To report gains or losses from real estate transactions

d) To report income from a partnership

21.Qualified dividends are taxed at which rate(s)?

a) Ordinary income tax rates b) 0%, 15%, or 20%, depending on the taxpayer's income

c) A flat rate of 15% d) A flat rate of 20%

22.Which of the following types of income is taxable?

a) Child support payments

b) Inheritance

c) Alimony payments received under a divorce/separation agreement executed after 2018

d) Gifts from family

23.The sale of a principal residence may exclude up to how much in capital gains if filing status is Married Filing Jointly?

a) $250,000 b) $300,000 c) $400,000 d) $500,000

24. Which of the following is true about the taxation of Social Security benefits?

a) They are always tax-free

b) They are taxed at a flat rate of 10%

c) A portion may be taxable depending on other income

d) They are fully taxable at ordinary income rates

25.When might a taxpayer use Form 6251, Alternative Minimum Tax?

a) To report income from investments

b) To calculate an alternative minimum tax amount

c) To report income from a partnership

d) To report income from rental property

26.What is the primary purpose of Form 1099-CAP, Changes in Corporate Control and Capital Structure?

a) To report income from investments

b) To report changes in corporate control or capital structure

c) To report income from a partnership

d) To report income from rental property

27.Which form is used to report income from bartering?

a) Form 1099-B b) Form 1099-G c) Form 1099-MISC d) Form 1099-K

28.When might a taxpayer use Form 2439, Notice to Shareholder of Undistributed Long-Term Capital Gains?

a) To report income from investments

b) To report undistributed long-term capital gains from a mutual fund

c) To report income from a partnership d) To report income from rental property

29.What type of income is reported on Form 1099-INT?

A. Dividend income B. Interest income C. Capital gains D. Rental income

30.What is the primary purpose of Form 4684, Casualties and Thefts?

a) To report income from investments b) To report losses from casualties or thefts

c) To report income from a partnership d) To report income from rental property

31.What tax form is used to report income from canceled debts that exceed $600?

a) Form 1099-C b) Form 1099-NEC c) Form 1040 d) Form W-2G

32.When might a taxpayer use Form 1099-Q, Payments From Qualified Education Programs?

a) To report income from investments

b) To report payments from qualified education programs

c) To report income from rental property

d) To report income from a partnership

33. Which form is issued to taxpayers to report payments from pension, retirement, or profit-sharing plans?

a) Form 1099-R b) Form 1040

c) Schedule K-1 d) Form W-2

34.How is the cost basis of a sold asset typically determined?

a) Original purchase price plus improvements

b) Current market value at the time of sale

c) Appraised value for tax purposes

d) Original purchase price only

35.When might a taxpayer use Form 1099-QA, Distributions from ABLE Accounts?

a) To report income from investments

b) To report distributions from ABLE accounts

c) To report income from rental property

d) To report income from a partnership

36.Which tax form is used to report income from alimony received?

a) Form 1099-NEC b) Form 1040 c) Form W-2 d) Form 1099-MISC

37.What is the primary purpose of Form 1099-LS, Reportable Policy Sale Information?

a) To report income from investments

b) To report changes in income to the IRS

c) To report information about reportable policy sales

d) To report income from rental property

38.When might a taxpayer use Form 1099-A, Acquisition or Abandonment of Secured Property?

a) To report income from investments

b) To report acquisition or abandonment of secured property

c) To report income from rental property

d) To report income from a partnership

39. What is the maximum amount of capital loss that can be deducted against ordinary income in one year?

a) $1,500

b) $2,000

c) $3,000

d) $3,500

40. What is the Section 179 deduction?

a) A deduction for personal expenses

b) A special depreciation allowance for real estate

c) An immediate expense deduction businesses can take for purchases of depreciable business equipment

d) A deduction for medical expenses exceeding a certain percentage of income

Part I - Section 3: Deductions and Credits

1.Mortgage insurance premiums paid in connection with acquisition debt for a qualified residence are:

a) Not deductible

b) Deductible as mortgage interest to the extent they exceed 2% of AGI

c) Fully deductible as an itemized deduction

d) Deductible only if paid before January 1, 2021

2.Which form is used to claim the Child and Dependent Care Credit?

a) Form 1040 b) Schedule C (Form 1040) c) Form 2441 d) Form 1098-T

3.What is the primary purpose of Form 8917, Tuition and Fees Deduction?

a) To report income from investments

b) To claim a deduction for tuition and fees paid for higher education

c) To report income from rental property

d) To report income from a partnership

4.When might a taxpayer use Form 8396, Mortgage Interest Credit?

a) To report income from investments

b) To claim a credit for mortgage interest paid

c) To report income from rental property

d) To report income from a partnership

5.Which document is used to claim the Earned Income Credit?

a) Form 1040

b) Form W-2

c) Form 1098-E

d) Schedule EIC (Form 1040)

6.Contributions made to a qualified charitable organization can be deducted up to what percentage of the taxpayer's AGI?

a) 30% b) 50% c) 60% d) There is no limit

7.When might a taxpayer use Form 8880, Credit for Qualified Retirement Savings Contributions?

a) To claim a credit for retirement savings contributions

b) To report income from investments

c) To report income from rental property

d) To report income from a partnership

8.Which form is used to claim the Lifetime Learning Credit?

a) Form 1040 b) Schedule C (Form 1040) c) Form 8863 d) Form 1098-T

9.What is the primary purpose of Form 8885, Health Coverage Tax Credit?

a) To report income from investments b) To claim a credit for health coverage premiums c) To report income from rental property d) To report income from a partnership

10.When might a taxpayer use Schedule A (Form 1040), Itemized Deductions?

a) To report income from investments

b) To claim itemized deductions rather than the standard deduction

c) To report income from rental property

d) To report income from a partnership

11.Which form is used to claim the Child Tax Credit?

a) Form 1040 b) Form W-2 c) Form 8862 d) Schedule 8812 (Form 1040)

12.Which of the following is not an itemized deduction?

a) State and local taxes paid

b) Mortgage interest

c) Work-related education expenses

d) Charitable contributions

13.When might a taxpayer use Form 8867, Paid Preparer's Earned Income Credit Checklist?

a) To report income from investments b) To claim the Earned Income Credit

c) To report income from rental property d) To report income from a partnership

14.Which of the following educational expenses is eligible for the tuition and fees deduction?

a) Room and board b) Transportation

c) Tuition and enrollment fees d) Personal living expenses

15.The Adoption Credit is a nonrefundable credit that covers qualified adoption expenses up to (for 2023):

a) $10,000 b) $13,810 c) $14,300 d) $15,950

16.When might a taxpayer use Form 8888, Allocation of Refund?

a) To report income from investments b) To allocate a tax refund into multiple accounts c) To report income from rental property d) To report income from a partnership

17.Which form is used to claim the Retirement Savings Contributions Credit?

a) Form 8880 b) Form 1098-T c) Form 8962 d) Form 8822

18.The American Opportunity Tax Credit is partially refundable up to what amount?

a) $1,000 b) $1,500 c) $2,500 d) None of the above

19.When might a taxpayer use Form 8995, Qualified Business Income Deduction Simplified Computation?

a) To report income from investments

b) To claim the qualified business income deduction

c) To report income from rental property

d) To report income from a partnership

20.The Foreign-Earned Income Exclusion allows taxpayers to exclude income earned abroad up to:

a) $102,100 b) $105,900 c) $107,600 d) $108,700

21.What is the primary purpose of Form 8812, Additional Child Tax Credit?

a) To report income from investments b) To claim an additional child tax credit

c) To report income from rental property d) To report income from a partnership

22.When might a taxpayer use Form 1040X, Amended U.S. Individual Income Tax Return?

a) To report income from investments b) To amend a previously filed tax return

c) To report income from rental property d) To report income from a partnership

23. The Residential Energy Efficient Property Credit includes which of the following?

a) Costs of installing energy-efficient windows only

b) Costs of Solar Electric Property and Solar Water Heaters

d) Costs of purchasing fuel-efficient vehicles

d) All of the above

24.What is the primary purpose of Form 1098-E, Student Loan Interest Statement?

a) To report income from investments b) To report student loan interest paid

c) To report income from rental property d) To report income from a partnership

25.When might a taxpayer use Form 8936, Qualified Plug-in Electric Drive Motor Vehicle Credit?

a) To report income from investments

b) To claim a credit for a qualified plug-in electric drive motor vehicle

c) To report income from rental property

d) To report income from a partnership

26.Which of the following is a characteristic of the Lifetime Learning Credit?

a) It is limited to four years of post-secondary education. b) It is 100% refundable.

c) It can be used for undergraduate, graduate, and professional degree courses.

d) It covers expenses for books, supplies, and equipment required for coursework.

27.The Child and Dependent Care Credit is available for expenses incurred due to the care of:

a) Any dependent child under age 13

b) A spouse who is physically or mentally incapable of self-care

c) Both A and B d) Neither A nor B

28.When might a taxpayer use Form 8863, Education Credits (American Opportunity and Lifetime Learning Credits)?

a) To report income from investments

b) To claim education-related tax credits

c) To report income from rental property

d) To report income from a partnership

29.What is the standard deduction for a married couple filing jointly in 2024?

a) $29,400 b) $29,200 c) $28,100 d) $28,400

30. Medical and dental expenses are deductible to the extent that they exceed what percentage of the taxpayer's adjusted gross income (AGI)?

a) 7.5% b) 10% c) 15% d) 20%

31.For the tax year 2024, what is the maximum amount of contributions that can be deducted for an Individual Retirement Account (IRA) for those under age 50?

a) $5,500 b) $7,000 c) $6,500 d) $9,000

32. Which of the following is not considered a deductible business expense for a self-employed individual?

a) Home office expenses b) Personal health insurance premiums

c) Entertainment expenses related to business d) Advertising costs

33.What is the primary purpose of Form 8815, Exclusion of Interest from Series EE and I U.S. Savings Bonds?

a) To report income from investments b) To exclude interest from certain savings bonds c) To report income from rental property d) To report income from a partnership

34.When might a taxpayer use Form 8283, Noncash Charitable Contributions?

a) To report income from investments

b) To claim deductions for noncash charitable contributions

c) To report income from rental property

d) To report income from a partnership

35.Which credit is available to eligible individuals or families with qualifying children under the age of 17?

a) Earned Income Tax Credit b) Child Tax Credit

c) American Opportunity Tax Credit d) Lifetime Learning Credit

36.What is the primary purpose of Form 5695, Residential Energy Credits?

a) To report income from investments b) To claim residential energy efficiency tax credits c) To report income from rental property d) To report income from a partnership

37.When might a taxpayer use Form 8288, U.S. Withholding Tax Return for Dispositions by Foreign Persons of U.S. Real Property Interests?

a) To report income from investments

b) To report withholding tax on dispositions of U.S. real property interests

c) To report income from rental property

d) To report income from a partnership

38.The Earned Income Tax Credit (EITC) is designed to benefit individuals and families who:

a) Have investment income above $3,650

b) Earn income from self-employment only

c) Have earned income and adjusted gross income within certain limits

d) Are over the age of 65

39.What is the primary purpose of Form 8910, Alternative Motor Vehicle Credit?

a) To report income from investments

b) To claim a credit for alternative motor vehicle purchases

c) To report income from rental property

d) To report income from a partnership

40.When might a taxpayer use Form 8606, Nondeductible IRAs?

a) To report income from investments

b) To track nondeductible IRA contributions

c) To report income from rental property

d) To report income from a partnership

Part I - Section 4: Taxation and Advice

1.What is the primary purpose of Form 945, Annual Return of Withheld Federal Income Tax?

a) To report income from investments

b) To report withholding of federal income tax on non-payroll payments

c) To report income from rental property

d) To report income from a partnership

2.When might a taxpayer use Form 1099-MISC, Miscellaneous Income?

a) To report income from investments

b) To report income from rental property

c) To report miscellaneous income not included on other information returns

d) To report income from a partnership

3.What is the highest tax rate for capital gains in 2024?

A. 15% B. 20% C. 25% D. 28%

4.What is the primary purpose of Form 1099-NEC, Nonemployee Compensation?

a) To report income from investments

b) To report nonemployee compensation exceeding $600

c) To report income from rental property

d) To report income from a partnership

5.The Net Investment Income Tax (NIIT) applies at a rate of:

a) 2.9% b) 3.8% c) 0.9% d) 1.45%

6.Which of the following is not subject to federal income tax?

A. Unemployment compensation

B. Social Security benefits under certain conditions

C. Life insurance proceeds

D. Alimony received under a decree executed after 2018

7.What is the primary purpose of Form 8300, Report of Cash Payments Over $10,000 Received in a Trade or Business?

a) To report income from investments

b) To report cash payments exceeding $10,000 received in a trade or business

c) To report income from rental property

d) To report income from a partnership

8.For 2024, what is the threshold for the estate tax exemption amount?

a) $5.49 million b). $13.61 million c) $10.00 million d) $3.50 million

9.Which form is used to report income from interest earned on a bank account?

a) Form 1099-DIV b) Form 1099-INT

c) Form 1099-MISC d) Form 1099-B

10.Which of the following deductions is allowed in calculating the Alternative Minimum Tax (AMT)?

a) State and local tax deductions

b) Standard deduction

c) Medical expenses above 10% of AGI

d) Personal exemptions

11.When might a taxpayer use Form 4852, Substitute for Form W-2 or 1099-R?

a) To report income from investments

b) To substitute for a missing or incorrect Form W-2 or 1099-R

c) To report income from rental property

d) To report income from a partnership

12. What is the purpose of Form W-2G?

a) To report gambling winnings

b) To report earnings from self-employment

c) To report distributions from pensions and annuities

d) To report interest and dividends

13.What is the primary purpose of Form 1099-R, Distributions from Pensions, Annuities, Retirement or Profit-Sharing Plans, IRAs, Insurance Contracts, etc.?

a) To report income from investments

b) To report distributions from various retirement or pension plans

c) To report income from rental property

d) To report income from a partnership

14.When might a taxpayer use Form 1116, Foreign Tax Credit?

a) To report income from investments

b) To claim a credit for taxes paid to foreign countries

c) To report income from rental property d) To report income from a partnership

15. The Foreign Tax Credit is intended to help taxpayers avoid:

a) Estate tax b) Double taxation on foreign income

c) Alternative Minimum Tax d) Self-employment tax

16.What is the primary purpose of Form 4506-T, Request for Transcript of Tax Return?

a) To report income from investments

b) To request a transcript of a previously filed tax return

c) To report income from rental property d) To report income from a partnership

17.When might a taxpayer use Form 1096, Annual Summary and Transmittal of U.S. Information Returns?

a) To report income from investments

b) To summarize and transmit various information returns to the IRS

c) To report income from rental property d) To report income from a partnership

18. Which of the following statements about the Affordable Care Act (ACA) tax provisions is correct?

a) All individuals are required to maintain minimum essential coverage or pay a penalty.

b) The penalty for not having health insurance was increased in 2020.

c) The penalty for not having health insurance was eliminated in 2019 for federal taxes. d) Employers with less than 50 full-time employees must provide health insurance.

19.What is the primary purpose of Form 1040-ES, Estimated Tax for Individuals?

a) To report income from investments

b) To estimate and pay quarterly taxes for individuals with income not subject to withholding

c) To report income from rental property

d) To report income from a partnership

20.When might a taxpayer use Form 8965, Health Coverage Exemptions?

a) To report income from investments

b) To claim exemptions from health coverage requirements

c) To report income from rental property

d) To report income from a partnership

21. Kiddie Tax applies to the unearned income of certain children. What is the age limit for the Kiddie Tax to apply if the child is a full-time student?

a) 18 b) 19 c) 24 d) 21

22. How is the child tax credit for the 2023 tax year treated if it exceeds the taxpayer's tax liability?

A. The excess is refunded up to $1,600 per qualifying child as the additional child tax credit.

B. The entire amount is refundable.

C. The excess is carried forward to the next tax year.

D. Only a portion determined by the taxpayer's income is refundable.

23. Backup withholding may be required on certain payments. What is the standard rate for backup withholding?

a) 24% b) 28% c) 30% d) 15%

24. A taxpayer selling their primary residence can exclude capital gains if they have lived in the house for 2 out of the last 5 years. What is the maximum exclusion amount for a single filer?

a) $250,000 b) $500,000 c) $200,000 d) $400,000

25.What is the primary purpose of Form 1099-G, Certain Government Payments?

a) To report income from investments

b) To report certain government payments like unemployment compensation or state tax refunds

c) To report income from rental property

d) To report income from a partnership

26.When might a taxpayer use Form 1120, U.S. Corporation Income Tax Return?

a) To report income from investments

b) To report income from a corporation

c) To report income from rental property

d) To report income from a partnership

27.Taxpayers can exclude foreign-earned income up to a certain limit. What was the limit for the 2023 tax year (per person)?

a) $105,900

b) $108,700

c) $112,000

d) $120,000

28.What is the primary purpose of Form 1099-S, Proceeds from Real Estate Transactions?

a) To report income from investments

b) To report proceeds from real estate transactions exceeding $600

c) To report income from rental property

d) To report income from a partnership

29.When might a taxpayer use Form 720, Quarterly Federal Excise Tax Return?

a) To report income from investments

b) To report excise taxes on specific goods, services, and activities

c) To report income from rental property

d) To report income from a partnership

30.Taxpayers receiving dividends from U.S. corporations are subject to tax. Which of the following types of dividends are taxed at preferential capital gains tax rates?

a) Ordinary dividends b) Non-qualified dividends

c) Qualified dividends d) All dividends are taxed at the same rate

31.Which of the following is not a characteristic of the Alternative Minimum Tax (AMT)?

a) It ensures that high-income individuals pay a minimum amount of tax.

b) It allows for the deduction of personal exemptions.

c) It disallows some deductions allowed for regular tax purposes.

d) It uses a separate set of rules to calculate taxable income.

32.When might a taxpayer use Form 941, Employer's Quarterly Federal Tax Return?

a) To report income from investments

b) To report quarterly employment taxes

c) To report income from rental property

d) To report income from a partnership

33.When must taxpayers make their final estimated tax payment for the year 2024?

a) January 15, 2025 b) April 15, 2025 c) December 31, 2024 d) June 15, 2024

34.What is the primary purpose of Form 1098, Mortgage Interest Statement?

a) To report income from investments

b) To report mortgage interest paid by an individual

c) To report income from rental property

d) To report income from a partnership

35.The adoption credit is a nonrefundable credit that helps with the expenses of adopting a child. For 2023, what is the maximum amount of the credit per child?

a) $10,000 b) $13,810 c) $14,300 d) $15,950

36.The penalty for failure to file a tax return is usually what percentage of the unpaid taxes for each month or part of a month the return is late?

a) 0.5% b) 1% c) 5% d) 10%

37.What is the primary purpose of Form W-4, Employee's Withholding Certificate?

a) To report income from investments

b) To specify the amount of federal income tax to be withheld from an employee's paycheck

c) To report income from rental property

d) To report income from a partnership

38.When might a taxpayer use Form 7004, Application for Automatic Extension of Time to File Certain Business Income Tax, Information, and Other Returns?

a) To report income from investments

b) To request an extension for certain business income tax returns

c) To report income from rental property

d) To report income from a partnership

39.Which of the following income levels would subject a taxpayer to the Additional Medicare Tax?

a) $150,000 for married filing jointly

b) $125,000 for single filers

c) $200,000 for single filers

d) $250,000 for head of household

40.Which of the following taxpayers would likely be subject to the Kiddie Tax?

a) A 20-year-old full-time college student with unearned income of $2,500

b) A 25-year-old graduate student with unearned income of $1,200

c) A 17-year-old high school student with earned income of $3,000

d) A 22-year-old who is not a student with unearned income of $1,000

41.When might a taxpayer use Form 8822, Change of Address?

a) To report income from investments

b) To notify the IRS of a change of address

c) To report income from rental property

d) To report income from a partnership

42.Which of the following incomes is subject to self-employment tax?

a) Interest income from personal savings

b) Dividend income

c) Net earnings from self-employment

d) Unemployment compensation

43.The Additional Medicare Tax applies to individuals who exceed a certain income threshold. What is the rate of this tax?

a) 0.9%

b) 1.45%

c) 2.35%

d) 3.8%

44.When might a taxpayer use Form 5498, IRA Contribution Information?

a) To report income from investments

b) To report contributions made to an IRA

c) To report income from rental property

d) To report income from a partnership

45.For which of the following statuses is the "Married Filing Jointly" standard deduction amount in 2024 doubled compared to the "Single" filer?

a) Single

b) Married Filing Separately

c) Head of Household

d) Qualifying Widow(er)

Part I - Section 5: Advising the Individual Taxpayer

1.When might a taxpayer use Form 2441, Child and Dependent Care Expenses?
a) To report income from investments
b) To claim a credit for child and dependent care expenses
c) To report income from rental property d) To report income from a partnership

2.What is the primary purpose of Form 8962, Premium Tax Credit (PTC)?
a) To report income from investments b) To reconcile and claim the premium tax credit
c) To report income from rental property d) To report income from a partnership

3.Which form is used to report distributions from an HSA, Archer MSA, or Medicare Advantage MSA?
a) Form 1099-DIV b) Form 1099-INT c) Form 1099-SA d) Form 1099-B

4.What is the primary purpose of Form 8853, Archer MSAs and Long-Term Care Insurance Contracts?
a) To report income from investments
b) To report distributions from Archer MSAs and long-term care insurance contracts
c) To report income from rental property
d) To report income from a partnership

5.When advising a taxpayer who works from home, which of the following expenses might be deductible as part of the home office deduction?
a) Groceries b)Mortgage interest and property taxes
c) Home renovation costs d) Commuting expenses

6.What is a critical consideration for taxpayers when deciding between itemizing deductions or taking the standard deduction?
a) The impact on state tax returns
b) Whether they have foreign income
c) Their filing status is married filing separately
d) The total amount of itemizable deductions exceeds the standard deduction

7.For individuals with high medical expenses, which tax planning strategy might be advisable?

a) Aggregating medical procedures into a single tax year to exceed the AGI threshold for deduction

b) Distributing medical expenses evenly over several years

c) Electing not to claim medical expenses as deductions to avoid AMT

d) Only claiming medical insurance premiums to stay below the deduction cap.

8.When advising a client on the tax benefits of higher education costs, which of the following credits is specifically designed to support undergraduate education expenses?

a) Lifetime Learning Credit b) American Opportunity Tax Credit

c) Education Savings Account d) Tuition and Fees Deduction

9.Which of the following is an appropriate strategy for taxpayers looking to reduce their taxable estate?

a) Investing in tax-exempt municipal bonds

b) Making annual gifts up to the federal gift tax exclusion limit

c) Converting all assets into cash d) Deferring all income into the next tax year

10.What is the primary purpose of Form 1099-INT?

a) To report income from investments b) To report interest income earned during the tax year c) To report income from rental property d) To report income from a partnership

11.When might a taxpayer use Form 4684, Casualties and Thefts?

a) To report income from investments b) To claim a deduction for casualty and theft losses

c) To report income from rental property d) To report income from a partnership

12.A taxpayer interested in saving for retirement while reducing taxable income should consider contributing to:

a) A Roth IRA b) A traditional IRA c) A regular savings account d) A non-deductible IRA.

13.When advising a taxpayer about the tax implications of an early distribution from a retirement plan, which of the following is true?

a) The distribution is always tax-free b) The distribution may be subject to a 10% early withdrawal penalty c) The distribution can only be taxed at the state level
d) The taxpayer can always roll over the distribution into another retirement account without any tax implications

14.When might a taxpayer use Form 8880, Credit for Qualified Retirement Savings Contributions?
a) To report income from investments
b) To claim a credit for qualified retirement savings contributions
c) To report income from rental property d) To report income from a partnership

15.Which form is used to report income from the sale of a principal residence?
a) Form 1040 b) Form 1099-S c) Form 1099-B d) Form 1099-MISC

16.When might a taxpayer use Form 8915-E, Qualified 2020 Disaster Retirement Plan Distributions and Repayments?
a) To report income from investments b) To report qualified disaster-related retirement plan distributions c) To report income from rental property d) To report income from a partnership

17.Advising a taxpayer who wishes to claim a relative as a dependent, you inform them that the dependent must:
a) Be a U.S. citizen or resident b) Have lived with the taxpayer all year
c) Not have any income d) Be under the age of 18

18.What is the primary purpose of Form 5695, Residential Energy Credits?
a) To report income from investments b) To claim residential energy-efficient property credits c) To report income from rental property d) To report income from a partnership

19.When might a taxpayer use Form 8960, Net Investment Income Tax?
a) To report income from investments
b) To report net investment income subject to the Net Investment Income Tax
c) To report income from rental property d) To report income from a partnership

20.To advise a client on reducing taxable income through charitable giving, you suggest:
a) Donating appreciated stock held for more than one year to avoid capital gains tax
b) Giving only cash to ensure a full deduction
c) Donating to foreign charities
d) Limiting charitable contributions to 10% of their income

21.What is the primary purpose of Form 1099-Q, Payments From Qualified Education Programs?
a) To report income from investments
b) To report distributions from education savings accounts
c) To report income from rental property d) To report income from a partnership

22.A self-employed taxpayer seeking advice on reducing their taxable income might be encouraged to:
a) Reduce their business expenses b) Contribute to a SEP IRA
c) Increase their salary d) Elect corporate tax status for their business

23.A taxpayer considering converting a traditional IRA to a Roth IRA should be informed that:
a) The conversion will result in a penalty b) The converted amount is not taxable
c) The converted amount is taxable in the year of the conversion
d) Conversions are only allowed for high-income taxpayers

24.What is the primary purpose of Form 8829, Expenses for Business Use of Your Home?
a) To report income from investments b) To claim deductions for business use of a home
c) To report income from rental property d) To report income from a partnership

25.When might a taxpayer use Form 8889, Health Savings Accounts (HSAs)?
a) To report income from investments
b) To report contributions and distributions from an HSA
c) To report income from rental property
d) To report income from a partnership

26.When advising on the tax implications of selling a primary residence, which factor is crucial for excluding capital gains?
a) The home was the taxpayer's primary residence for at least 5 years
b) The home was the taxpayer's primary residence for at least 2 of the last 5 years
c) The sale price was under $250,000 d) The taxpayer is over the age of 65

27.What is the primary purpose of Form 8949, Sales and Other Dispositions of Capital Assets?
a) To report income from investments
b) To report gains or losses from the sale of capital assets
c) To report income from rental property d) To report income from a partnership

28.When discussing education savings options with a client, which feature is unique to a 529 plan compared to an ESA (Education Savings Account)?
A. Earnings grow tax-free if used for qualified education expenses
B. Contributions are tax-deductible C. There are higher contribution limits
D. Funds can only be used for post-secondary education

29. For a high-income client, which investment strategy could DIRECTLY minimize exposure to the Net Investment Income Tax (NIIT)?
a) Investing in municipal bonds
b) Maximizing contributions to tax-deferred retirement accounts
c) Investing in high-dividend stocks d) Increasing their holdings in real estate investments

30.What is Form 8332 crucial for?
a) Reporting foreign income
b) Calculating self-employment tax
c) Determining which parent can claim a child as a dependent
d) Filing for an extension of time to file a tax return

31.When might a taxpayer use Form 8839, Qualified Adoption Expenses?
a) To report income from investments b) To claim expenses related to adopting a child
c) To report income from rental property d) To report income from a partnership

32.A client interested in the tax implications of an investment property should be advised that:
a) Losses can always be deducted in full against ordinary income b) Rental income is tax-free if the property is not rented out full-time c) Expenses and depreciation can offset rental income d) Capital gains tax does not apply to the sale of investment properties

33.In advising a client on charitable contributions, which of the following contributions would typically offer a tax deduction? a) Contributions to a political campaign
b) Contributions to an individual's GoFundMe campaign c) Contributions to a qualified nonprofit organization d) Contributions of services to a nonprofit organization

34.For a taxpayer interested in minimizing their tax liability through investment decisions, which of the following strategies is generally effective? a) Investing in high-yield bonds b) Holding investments long-term to qualify for capital gains treatment c) Trading securities frequently to realize short-term capital gains d) Investing primarily in collectibles

35.Taxpayers can avoid the underpayment penalty for estimated taxes if they pay:
a. 90% of the current year's tax liability b. 100% of the prior year's tax liability
c. The minimum required quarterly payment d. A and B

36.When advising on estate planning, what is one strategy to reduce estate tax liability?
a) Gifting assets up to the annual exclusion amount each year to family members
b) Accumulating assets in the taxpayer's estate c) Avoiding the creation of a will
d) Consolidating all assets into a single checking account

37.When might a taxpayer use Form 6251, Alternative Minimum Tax - Individuals? a) To report income from investments b) To calculate alternative minimum tax liability c) To report income from rental property d) To report income from a partnership

38.When discussing health savings accounts (HSAs) with a taxpayer, it is important to highlight that contributions: a) Are not tax-deductible b) Can only be used for cosmetic procedures c) Are tax-deductible and withdrawals for qualified medical expenses are tax-free d) Must be used by the end of the year or be forfeited

39.A client receives a large bonus at the end of the year and wants to reduce their tax liability. What could you recommend?

a) Deferring the bonus to the next tax year b) Increasing their 401(k) contributions
c) Gifting the entire bonus to a family member d)Investing the bonus in a traditional IRA

40.A taxpayer looking to invest in education savings for their child should be informed about the benefits of:

a) A traditional IRA b) A Roth IRA c) A 529 plan d) A life insurance policy.

41.Advising a client on dividend income, you explain that qualified dividends are taxed at:

a) Ordinary income rates b) Preferential capital gains rates
c) A flat rate of 30% d) A flat rate of 10%

42.What is the primary purpose of Form 8582, Passive Activity Loss Limitations?

a) To report income from investments
b) To calculate and report passive activity loss limitations
c) To report income from rental property
d) To report income from a partnership

43.When advising a client on tax-saving strategies for retirement planning, which account type do you recommend for tax-deferred growth?

a) Traditional IRA b) Roth IRA c) Regular brokerage account d) Checking account

44.How can taxpayers avoid underpayment penalties for estimated taxes?

a) Pay at least 90% of the tax for the current year b) Pay 100% of the tax shown on the prior year's return c) Adjust withholdings to cover the tax liability d)All of the above

45.What advice would you give to a client who has multiple sources of income and wants to avoid owing taxes at year-end?

a) Reduce the number of allowances claimed on their W-4
b) Convert all earnings to nontaxable income
c) Stop withholding taxes from their paychecks
d) Only report their primary source of income on their tax return

Part I - Section 6: Specialized Returns for Individuals

1.When might a taxpayer use Form 2555?

a) To report income from investments b) To claim the foreign-earned income exclusion

c) To report income from rental property d) To report income from a partnership

2.The Residential Energy Credits are claimed on Form:

a) 5695 b) 8863 c) 2441 d) 8880

3.Form 1040-SR is designed for:

a) Self-employed individuals.

b) Students reporting education credits.

c) Taxpayers age 65 or older.

d) Nonresident aliens.

4.When might a taxpayer use Form 6252, Installment Sale Income?

a) To report income from investments

b) To report installment sale income from selling property

c) To report income from rental property

d) To report income from a partnership

5.Which document is used to report income from farming activities?

a) Form 1099-NEC b) Form 1099-G c) Schedule F (Form 1040) d) Form 1099-MISC

6.Which form is used by individuals to amend a previously filed tax return?

a) Form 1040 b) Form 1040-X c) Form 1040-ES d) Form 1040-SR

7.When might a taxpayer use Form 3468, Investment Credit?

a) To report income from investments

b) To claim credits for investment in certain qualified properties

c) To report income from rental property

d) To report income from a partnership

8.Form 2848 is used for granting:

a) Power of attorney

b) Authorization to release tax information

c) Consent to extend the time to assess tax

d) Permission to apply for an ITIN

9.A taxpayer would file Form 3903 to deduct:

a) Moving expenses for members of the Armed Forces

b) Job search expenses

c) Unreimbursed employee expenses

d) Home office expenses

10.When might a taxpayer use Form 8814, Parent's Election To Report Child's Interest and Dividends?

a) To report income from investments

b) To report a child's interest and dividend income on the parent's return

c) To report income from rental property

d) To report income from a partnership

11.The Adoption Credit is claimed on Form:

a) 8839 b) 8862 c) 8919 d) 8949

12.What is the primary purpose of Form 6198, At-Risk Limitations?

a) To report income from investments

b) To calculate and report at-risk limitations for certain activities

c) To report income from rental property

d) To report income from a partnership

13.U.S. citizens living abroad can use Form 2555 to claim:

a) Additional child tax credit

b) Foreign-earned income exclusion.

c) Education credits

d) First-time homebuyer credit.

14.Form 4868 is used to:

a) Amend a tax return. b) Request an automatic extension to file.

c) Report self-employment income. d) Pay estimated taxes.

15.The tax form used by a nonresident alien individual to report U.S. income is:

a) Form 1040-NR. b) Form 1040. c) Form W-8BEN. d) Form 8833.

16.When might a taxpayer use Form 8833, Treaty-Based Return Position Disclosure Under Section 6114 or 7701(b)?

a) To report income from investments

b) To disclose a position taken on a tax treaty

c) To report income from rental property

d) To report income from a partnership

17.Which form is used to report income from the sale of a business or capital assets?

a) Form 1099-NEC b) Form 1099-G c) Schedule D (Form 1040) d) Form 1099-MISC

18.Which form is used by individuals to voluntarily report previously undisclosed offshore financial accounts and assets?

a) Form 8938 b) FinCEN Form 114 (FBAR) c) Form 2555 d) Form 4868

19.Form 8814 is utilized when parents elect to:

a) Claim a child's unearned income on their tax return.

b) Release a claim to a child's exemption.

c) Deduct education expenses for a dependent.

d) Report a child's foreign income.

20.Form 5405 is related to:

a) First-Time Homebuyer Credit.

b) Renewable Energy Credit.

c) Adoption Credit.

d) Health Coverage Tax Credit.

21.What is the primary purpose of Form 8283, Noncash Charitable Contributions?

a) To report income from investments

b) To report noncash charitable contributions

c) To report income from rental property

d) To report income from a partnership

22.When might a taxpayer use Form 8615, Tax for Certain Children Who Have Investment Income of More Than $2,200?

a) To report income from investments

b) To calculate and report tax for children with significant investment income

c) To report income from rental property

d) To report income from a partnership

23.Form 8615 is required when:

a) A child has unearned income above a certain threshold.

b) Filing for the foreign-earned income exclusion.

c) Claiming the standard deduction.

d) Reporting tips received.

24.What is the primary purpose of Form 2553, Election by a Small Business Corporation?

a) To report income from investments

b) To elect to be treated as an S corporation for tax purposes

c) To report income from rental property

d) To report income from a partnership

25.When might a taxpayer use Form 8865, Return of U.S. Persons With Respect to Certain Foreign Partnerships?

a) To report income from investments

b) To report information about a foreign partnership interest

c) To report income from rental property

d) To report income from a partnership

26. Victims of federally declared disasters can claim casualty losses on:
a) Schedule A (Form 1040) b) Form 4684
c) Schedule E (Form 1040) d) Both A and B

27.What is the primary purpose of Form 5471, Information Return of U.S. Persons With Respect to Certain Foreign Corporations?
a) To report income from investments
b) To report information about certain foreign corporations
c) To report income from rental property d) To report income from a partnership

28.Form 8332 is related to:
a) Release/revocation of the release of claim to exemption for a child by the custodial parent
b) Earned Income Credit
c) Education Credits d) Health Coverage Exemptions

29.Taxpayers who receive income from a farming activity report their income and expenses on:
a) Form 1040 Schedule F b) Form 1040 Schedule A c) Form 4835 d) Form 2210-F

30.Which form do taxpayers use to report income from a rental property?
a) Schedule C b) Schedule E c) Schedule A d) Form 8829

31.When might a taxpayer use Form 8891, U.S. Information Return for Beneficiaries of Certain Canadian Registered Retirement Plans?
a) To report income from investments
b) To disclose information about certain Canadian retirement plans
c) To report income from rental property
d) To report income from a partnership

32.Which form is used to report income from a grantor trust?
a) Form 1099-NEC b) Form 1041
c) Form 1099-MISC d) Schedule D (Form 1040)

33. U.S. citizens living abroad can exclude a portion of their foreign-earned income using:
a) Form 2555 b) Form 1116 c) Form 8938 d) Schedule B (Form 1040)

34.The Foreign Tax Credit can be claimed on Form:
a) 1116 b) 2555 c) 1040-X d) 8822

35.Military reservists who travel more than 100 miles away from home and stay overnight for duties may deduct travel expenses on:
a) Form 2106 b) Schedule A (Form 1040) c) Form 1040, Line 24
d) They can no longer deduct these expenses due to changes in tax law

36.What is the primary purpose of Form 8233, Exemption From Withholding on Compensation for Independent (and Certain Dependent) Personal Services of a Nonresident Alien Individual?
a) To report income from investments
b) To claim an exemption from withholding on compensation for nonresident aliens
c) To report income from rental property
d) To report income from a partnership

37.Form 709 is used for reporting:
a) Gift taxes b) Income from farming activities
c) Additional Medicare Tax d) Net Investment Income Tax

38. Which form is used to calculate and report the self-employment tax?
a) Schedule SE b) Form 1040 Schedule C c) Form 2106 d) Schedule K-1 (Form 1065)

39.What is the primary purpose of Form 8300, Report of Cash Payments Over $10,000 Received in a Trade or Business?
a) To report income from investments
b) To report cash payments received over $10,000 in a trade or business
c) To report income from rental property
d) To report income from a partnership

40.When might a taxpayer use Form 8858, Information Return of U.S. Persons With Respect to Foreign Disregarded Entities?

a) To report income from investments

b) To report information about foreign disregarded entities

c) To report income from rental property

d) To report income from a partnership

41.The Alternative Minimum Tax (AMT) is calculated on which form?

a) Form 6251 b) Form 1040 Schedule A c) Form 8801 d) Schedule D

42.Taxpayers submit Form 5329 when they need to report:

a) Changes in address

b) Additional taxes on qualified plans

c) Foreign-earned income

d) Estimated tax payments

43.To claim a deduction for a home office, the space must be used:

a) Occasionally for business

b) Exclusively and regularly as your principal place of business

c) Primarily for employee meetings

d) As a convenience to your employer, without regularity

44.Which form is filed by individuals to report the sale or exchange of assets that are not capital assets?

a) Form 4797 b) Form 8949 c) Schedule D d) Form 6252

45.What is the primary purpose of Form 8960, Net Investment Income Tax—Individuals, Estates, and Trusts?

a) To report income from investments

b) To calculate and report net investment income tax

c) To report income from rental property

d) To report income from a partnership

PART 1

INDIVIDUALS

Fill in the Blank Questions

Part 1: Individuals
Fill in the blank questions

1. The due date for filing individual income tax returns (Form 1040) for the year 2023 is __________.

2. An individual taxpayer can claim a standard deduction in 2023 if they do not itemize deductions. For a single filer, the standard deduction amount is __________.

3. The maximum contribution amount to a traditional IRA for individuals under the age of 50 in 2023 is __________.

4. For the tax year 2023, the maximum amount of earned income credit (EIC) for a family with two children is __________.

5. The annual gift tax exclusion for 2023 is __________ per recipient.

6. Taxpayers over 65 or blind can claim an additional standard deduction amount. For a single taxpayer in 2023, this additional amount is __________.

7. The penalty for failure to file a tax return is typically __________ of the unpaid taxes for each month or part of a month that the return is late.

8. The maximum income limit for contributing to a Roth IRA for a single filer in 2023 is __________.

9. The American Opportunity Tax Credit (AOTC) maximum per eligible student per year is __________.

10. The maximum percentage of charitable cash contributions to public charities relative to adjusted gross income (AGI) in 2023 is __________.

11. The standard mileage rate for business use of a personal vehicle in 2023 is __________ cents per mile.

12. The Lifetime Learning Credit provides a maximum credit of __________ per tax return in 2023.

13. The Kiddie Tax applies to unearned income for children under age __________ and certain other conditions.

14. The threshold for mandatory health insurance coverage under the Affordable Care Act in 2023 is __________.

15. A qualifying relative for dependency exemption purposes must have a gross income less than __________ in 2023.

16. The phase-out range for deducting contributions to a traditional IRA for a married couple filing jointly, where the spouse making the IRA contribution is covered by a workplace retirement plan, starts at __________ in 2023.

17. The self-employment tax rate for 2023 is __________ of net earnings.

18. The adoption credit for 2023 is limited to a maximum amount of __________ per eligible child.

19. The Safe Harbor rule for avoiding a penalty for underpayment of estimated tax requires paying at least __________ of your current year tax liability or __________ of your prior year tax liability, whichever is smaller.

20. The maximum amount of qualified business income eligible for the 20% deduction under Section 199A in 2023 is __________ for single filers.

21. Taxpayers must report health savings account (HSA) distributions on Form __________.

22. The penalty for not maintaining minimum essential health coverage in 2023 is ________.

23. The education savings bond program allows taxpayers to exclude the interest from income if used for education expenses, with income phase-outs beginning at __________ for married filing jointly in 2023.

24. The maximum allowable expense for the Dependent Care Credit in 2023 for two or more qualifying persons is __________.

25. The threshold for the itemized deduction of medical and dental expenses is __________ of AGI for 2023.

26. Taxpayers aged 50 and over can make a catch-up contribution to their 401(k) of up to __________ in 2023.

27. The Qualified Business Income Deduction (Section 199A) is __________ of qualified business income for eligible taxpayers.

28. For 2023, the maximum amount of compensation considered for calculating contributions to defined contribution plans is __________.

29. The penalty for a bounced check to the IRS of $1,250 or more is __________ of the amount of the check.

30. The minimum age for making a qualified charitable distribution from an IRA directly to a charity is __________.

31. The limit on the exclusion for gain from the sale of a primary residence is __________ for singles and __________ for married couples filing jointly.

32. For 2023, the annual limit on contributions to a Health Savings Account (HSA) for family coverage is __________.

33. The maximum foreign housing exclusion for 2023 is __________.

34. An individual's capital loss carryover to the next year is limited to __________ per year if they have no capital gains.

35. The tax rate on net investment income under the Medicare Tax is __________.

36. For estate tax purposes, the basic exclusion amount in 2023 is __________.

37. The Child Tax Credit amount per qualifying child under the age of 17 for the tax year 2023 is __________.

38. The limit for elective deferrals into a SIMPLE IRA in 2024 for individuals under 50 is __________.

39. The maximum income for a single filer to qualify for the Retirement Savings Contributions Credit (Saver's Credit) in 2023 is __________.

40. The deduction for each exemption claimed on a tax return in 2023 is __________ (note: personal and dependency exemptions have been set to $0 since 2018 under the Tax Cuts and Jobs Act).

41. For the 2023 tax year, the long-term capital gains tax rate for a single filer with taxable income between $44,626 and $492,300 is __________.

42. The due date for a U.S. citizen living abroad to file their 2023 tax return is __________.

43. Taxpayers must begin taking Required Minimum Distributions (RMDs) from their retirement accounts at age __________ as of 2023.

44. The maximum exclusion for a qualified small business stock (QSBS) held for more than 5 years is __________ of the gain.

45. The dollar limit on the deduction for business meals expenses in 2023 is __________ of the cost.

46. The limit for elective deferrals into a SIMPLE IRA in 2023 for individuals under 50 is __________.

47. For 2023, the penalty for an individual who fails to report a foreign bank account is up to __________ of the account's highest balance.

48. The maximum credit for the Elderly or Disabled Credit for a single taxpayer in 2023 is __________.

49. The limit on annual contributions to a Coverdell Education Savings Account (ESA) per beneficiary in 2023 is __________.

50. The premium tax credit is available to individuals and families whose income is between __________ and __________ percent of the federal poverty line in 2023.

51. The income threshold for a single taxpayer to be ineligible for the Premium Tax Credit in 2023 is __________.

52. The deduction limit for contributions to a SEP IRA in 2023 is __________ of compensation or __________, whichever is less.

53. The tax year 2023 standard mileage rate for medical or moving purposes for qualified active duty members of the Armed Forces is __________ cents per mile.

54. The maximum contribution to a 529 plan in 2023 that qualifies for the annual gift tax exclusion is __________ per donor, per beneficiary.

55. The penalty rate applied to early distributions from an IRA or 401(k) plan before age 59½, unless an exception applies, is __________.

56. The maximum amount of debt forgiveness eligible for the Mortgage Forgiveness Debt Relief Act exclusion in 2023 is __________.

57. The exclusion from gross income for benefits received under an employer's educational assistance program in 2023 is up to __________.

58. The threshold amount for filing a tax return for a single individual under 65 in 2023 is __________.

59. The phase-out range for the student loan interest deduction for a single filer in 2023 begins at __________.

60. The maximum refundable portion of the Child Tax Credit per child in 2023 is __________.

61. The phase-out for the Lifetime Learning Credit for married filing jointly taxpayers starts at __________ in 2023.

62. The penalty for not filing Form 5471, Information Return of U.S. Persons With Respect To Certain Foreign Corporations, can be up to __________ per form.

63. For the tax year 2023, the maximum foreign tax credit without filing Form 1116, for individual taxpayers, is __________.

64. Taxpayers must keep their tax records for at least __________ years after filing the return.

65. The maximum age for a child to qualify for the Child and Dependent Care Credit is __________ years old.

66. The maximum amount of compensation that can be deferred under a 457(b) plan in 2023 is __________.

67. For 2023, the penalty for failing to file a Report of Foreign Bank and Financial Accounts (FBAR) on FinCEN Form 114 is up to __________, unless the failure was willful.

68. The limit for the exclusion of gain on the sale of qualified small business stock (QSBS) under Section 1202 for 2023 is __________ of the gain.

69. The personal casualty and theft loss deduction for tax year 2023 is only deductible to the extent that it is attributable to a federally declared __________.

70. The interest rate on underpayments and overpayments for the first quarter of 2024 is __________ percent per annum.

71. The minimum penalty for late filing of a tax return more than 60 days after the due date is __________ or the amount of tax due, whichever is less, for 2023.

72. For the 2023 tax year, the income phase-out range for Roth IRA contributions starts at __________ for married couples filing jointly.

73. The number of months for which the premium for COBRA continuation coverage may be eligible for a tax credit under certain circumstances is __________ months.

74. The annual limit on the deduction for an individual's combined contributions to traditional and Roth IRAs in 2023 is __________.

75. The Qualified Business Income (QBI) deduction phases out completely for single filers engaged in a specified service trade or business with taxable income over _______ in 2023.

76. The maximum amount of adjusted gross income for a head of household filer to receive the full Earned Income Credit with three or more qualifying children in 2023 is ______.

77. The maximum amount of the Foreign-Earned Income Exclusion plus the Foreign Housing Exclusion for a taxpayer in 2023 is __________.

78. The basic standard deduction for a married couple filing jointly in 2023 is __________.

79. For 2023, individuals aged 55 or older can make an additional catch-up contribution to a Health Savings Account (HSA) of __________.

80. The maximum amount an individual can contribute to a myRA before it must be rolled over into a traditional IRA is __________.

81. The maximum Earned Income Credit for taxpayers with no qualifying children in 2023 is __________.

82. The exclusion amount for gifts to a spouse who is not a U.S. citizen in 2023 is __________.

83. The limit for the small employer health insurance tax credit as a percentage of premiums paid in 2023 is __________ percent.

84. The minimum amount of tax owed that requires a taxpayer to make estimated tax payments in 2023 is __________.

85. The threshold for single taxpayers under 65 to be required to file a 2023 tax return if they are claimed as a dependent on another's return is more than __________.

86. The penalty for not filing Form 3520, Annual Return To Report Transactions With Foreign Trusts and Receipt of Certain Foreign Gifts, is __________ of the gross reportable amount.

87. The dollar limitation for elective deferrals to a 403(b) plan in 2023 is __________.

88. The maximum credit amount for the Residential Energy Efficient Property Credit in 2023 is __________ percent of the cost of qualified property.

89. The maximum amount of the Home Office Deduction using the simplified method in 2023 is __________.

90. The adjusted gross income limit for deducting moving expenses for members of the Armed Forces in 2023 is __________.

91. The mileage rate for charitable services driven in 2023 is __________ cents per mile.

92. The maximum amount of wages protected from a federal tax levy for a single taxpayer with one exemption in a weekly pay period in 2023 is __________.

93. The phase-out range for the deduction of interest on student loans for married filing jointly taxpayers begins at __________ in 2023.

94. The dollar limit on employee salary reductions for contributions to health flexible spending arrangements (FSAs) in 2023 is __________.

95. The Child and Dependent Care Credit is a percentage of qualifying expenses, which for the tax year 2023 ranges from 20% to __________ of eligible expenses, depending on adjusted gross income.

96. For 2023, the income phase-out for the Lifetime Learning Credit begins at $__________ for single filers and $__________ for married filing jointly.

97. For the 2023 tax year, the maximum Earned Income Credit (EIC) for a family with three or more qualifying children is $__________.

98. In 2023, the amount of investment income a taxpayer can have and still qualify for the Earned Income Credit is limited to $__________ or less.

99. Taxpayers aged 65 or older or who are blind receive an additional standard deduction of $__________ for single filers and $__________ for married filing jointly, per occurrence, in 2023.

100. For 2023, the Alternative Minimum Tax (AMT) exemption amount for a single filer is $__________.

101. The maximum amount of qualified education expenses that can be withdrawn tax-free from a 529 plan per beneficiary in 2023 is $__________ for tuition at an elementary or secondary school (K-12).

102. The penalty for a bounced check to the IRS of less than $1,250 in 2023 is $__________.

103. The failure-to-pay penalty for unpaid taxes reported on a filed tax return is __________% per month of the unpaid tax, up to a maximum of 25%.

104. The maximum age for a "qualifying child" dependent for the Child Tax Credit in 2023 is __________.

105. The maximum credit for the Retirement Savings Contributions Credit (Saver's Credit) for a single taxpayer in 2023 is $__________.

106. Taxpayers who convert a traditional IRA to a Roth IRA in 2023 must include the conversion as income, except for contributions that were __________.

107. In 2023, the threshold for miscellaneous itemized deductions subject to the 2% floor is $__________.

108. The IRS threshold for mandatory electronic filing of tax returns by tax preparers who expect to file more than __________ returns in 2023 is in place to encourage electronic filing.

109. The form used to determine the amount of taxes to withhold from an employee's paycheck is Form _______.

110. Form _______ is utilized to inform the IRS of a change in address.

111. The _______ deduction is a specific dollar amount that reduces the income on which you are taxed and varies according to your filing status.

112. Taxpayers must file a tax return if their income exceeds the standard deduction and personal exemption amounts, which are adjusted annually for _______.

113. Income from freelancing or contracting work is reported on Schedule _______.

114. _______ compensation is considered taxable income and must be reported on your tax return.

115. The Earned Income Tax Credit (EITC) is not available for individuals filing as _______ Filing Separately.

116. To qualify as a dependent, the person must pass several tests, including the Support Test and the Relationship Test, but not the _______ Test.

117. If a taxpayer discovers an error on their previously filed tax return, they should file Form _______ to amend the return.

118. A taxpayer with a qualifying child can file as _______ of Household if they meet certain criteria.

119. To reconcile advanced payments of the premium tax credit, taxpayers use Form _______.

120. Interest and dividends are considered _______ income and are not subject to Social Security and Medicare taxes.

121. The American Opportunity Tax Credit supports educational expenses for the first _______ years of post-secondary education.

122. To request an automatic extension of time to file their tax return, taxpayers submit Form _______.

123. The exclusion amount for gifts to a spouse who is not a U.S. citizen in 2024 is __________.

PART 2

BUSINESSES

MULTIPLE-CHOICE QUESTIONS

Part II - Section 1: Businesses

1.Which of the following entities allows its owners to have limited liability but is taxed similarly to a partnership?
a) S Corporation b) C Corporation
c) Limited Liability Company (LLC) d) Sole Proprietorship

2.Under which section of the Internal Revenue Code are S Corporations governed?
a) Section 1202 b) Section 1244 c) Section 1361 d) Section 263A

3.What is the maximum number of shareholders allowed in an S Corporation?
a) 75 b) 100 c) 150 d) 200

4.Which form is used by partnerships to report income, deductions, and other tax-related information?
a) Form 1120 b) Form 1065 c) Form 1120S d) Form 1040

5.Which tax year is commonly used by partnerships for reporting their income and expenses?
a) Calendar year b) Fiscal year c) Hybrid year d) Rolling year

6.What is the tax rate for long-term capital gains in a C Corporation?
a) 0% b) 15% c) 20% d) 25%

7.What is the primary advantage of a limited liability partnership (LLP) over a general partnership?
a) Flow-through taxation b) Limited liability protection for all partners
c) Unlimited number of partners allowed d) Ability to issue publicly traded shares

8.Which tax form is used by C Corporations to report their income, deductions, and corporate transactions?
a) Form 1120S b) Form 1040 c) Form 1120 d) Form 1065

9.Which entity typically uses a Schedule K-1 to report income, deductions, and credits allocated to its owners?
a) Sole Proprietorship b) C Corporation
c) Limited Liability Company (LLC) d) Partnership

10.A business entity's choice of classification for federal tax purposes can be changed by filing Form:
a) 1120 b) 8832 c) 2553 d) 1040X

11.What is the maximum number of shareholders allowed in a C Corporation?
a) Unlimited b) 100 c) 500 d) 1,000

12.Which of the following entities is considered a separate taxpayer, requiring the filing of its own tax return?
a) Sole Proprietorship b) General Partnership c) C Corporation d) S Corporation

13.What is the tax treatment of dividends received by a C Corporation from another domestic corporation?
a) Fully taxable b) Partially taxable
c) Exempt from taxation d) Taxable only if exceeding $50,000

14.Which type of business structure provides the least protection against personal liability for business debts?
a) C Corporation b) S Corporation
c) Limited Liability Company (LLC) d) Sole Proprietorship

15. The accumulated earnings tax applies to:
a) S Corporations b) C Corporations c) Partnerships d) LLCs

16. Businesses may deduct the cost of goods sold (COGS) if they:
a) Are service-based businesses. b) Manufacture products or purchase them for resale.
c) Only have digital products. d) Are non-profit organizations.

17.What is the tax treatment for a Limited Liability Company (LLC) by default?
a) It is taxed as a corporation b) It is taxed as a sole proprietorship
c) It is taxed as a partnership d) It is tax-exempt

18.In a partnership, which type of partner typically has limited liability?
a) General partner b) Silent partner c) Active partner d) Limited partner

19. A business that incurs a net operating loss (NOL) may:
a) Only carry the loss back to previous tax years.
b) Only carry the loss forward to future tax years.
c) Neither carry the loss back nor forward)
d) Carry the loss back or forward, depending on the tax laws in effect.

20.What is the primary advantage of an S Corporation?
a) Unlimited liability protection b) Pass-through taxation
c) No ownership restrictions d) Double taxation

21.Which of the following is a characteristic of a C Corporation?
a) Pass-through taxation b) Limited liability for shareholders
c) Limited number of shareholders d) Sole ownership

22.What is the tax rate for a C Corporation's income above $50,000?
a) 15% b) 21% c) 25% d) 35

23.What form is used to apply for an Employer Identification Number (EIN)?
a) Form W-9 b) Form SS-4 c) Form 1099 d) Form W-4

24. The self-employment tax rate is comprised of:
a) Only Social Security taxes. b) Only Medicare taxes.
c) Both Social Security and Medicare taxes.
d) Social Security, Medicare, and federal income taxes.

25.What is the primary purpose of the articles of incorporation for a corporation?
a) To identify shareholders b) To outline the company's bylaws
c) To establish the corporation with the state d) To distribute profits

26. Payroll taxes paid by employers include:
a) Federal income tax and FUTA b) FICA and FUTA c) Only FICA d) Only FUTA

27.In a partnership, what is the tax treatment for partners' income?
a) It is taxed only at the partnership level
b) It is taxed only at the individual partner level
c) It is not subject to taxation
d) It is taxed at both the partnership and individual levels

28. The qualified business income deduction (Section 199A) applies to income from:
a) C Corporations. b) S Corporations, partnerships, sole proprietorships, and LLCs.
c) Only sole proprietorships. d) Only LLCs.

29. A __________ is a tax levied on the manufacture, sale, or consumption of a particular good or service.
a) Payroll tax b) Income tax c) Excise tax d) Property tax

30.Which entity is considered a separate legal entity from its owners?
a) Sole proprietorship b) General partnership c) Limited liability company d) Corporation

31.A business entity that elects to be taxed as a corporation files Form:
a). 8832 b) 2553 c) 1040 d) 1120S

32.A limited partnership typically consists of:
a) Two or more general partners b) One general partner and one limited partner
c) A single partner managing all affairs d) Two or more limited partners

33. The penalty for failure to file Form 1099-NEC by the deadline can be up to $________ per form, depending on how late the form is filed.
a) 50 b) 100 c) 310 d) 550

34. A business can deduct the cost of business insurance as a(n) __________ expense.

a) Capitalized b) Depreciated c) Ordinary and necessary d) Amortized

35. The research and development (R&D) tax credit is intended to encourage businesses to:

a) Expand their operations overseas.

b) Invest in startup companies.

c) Increase spending on qualifying research activities.

d) Purchase new manufacturing equipment.

36.4. Which of the following is a characteristic of S Corporations?

a) They are taxed at the corporate level.

b) Income and losses are passed through to shareholders.

c) There is no limitation on the number of shareholders.

d) Non-resident aliens can be shareholders.

37. Businesses that operate internationally may benefit from forming a(n):

a) Domestic partnership b) Offshore corporation

c) Employee Stock Ownership Plan (ESOP) d) Professional Corporation (PC)

38.In a C corporation, who typically manages the daily operations?

a) Shareholders b) Officers

c) Directors d) Partners

39.A Limited Liability Company (LLC) provides:

a) Unlimited liability for all members b) Pass-through taxation like an S Corporation

c) No protection against lawsuits d) Taxation at the corporate level only

40. Form 4562 is used for:

a) Reporting foreign bank and financial accounts.

b) Calculating and reporting depreciation and amortization.

c) Claiming the foreign tax credit.

d) Reporting income from a trust or estate.

41.At what ownership percentage does an individual become a controlling shareholder in a corporation?

a) 50% b) 51% c) 75% d) 100%

42.How is a Limited Liability Partnership (LLP) taxed?

a) As a corporation b) As a partnership

c) As a sole proprietorship d) As a disregarded entity

43. The use of an accounting method that records income when it is earned and expenses when they are incurred is known as the __________ method.

a) Cash b) Accrual c) Hybrid d) Modified cash

44.Pass-through taxation means:

a) Income is taxed only once at the corporate level

b) Income is taxed at both the corporate and individual levels

c) Income is taxed only at the individual level

d) Income is not subject to taxation

45.What tax form do S Corporations use to report income and expenses?

a) Form 1120 b) Form 1065 c) Form 1040 d) Form 1120S

46.Limited Liability Companies (LLCs) with only one member are treated as __________ for tax purposes unless they elect otherwise.

a) Corporations b) Disregarded entities c) Partnerships d) S Corporations

47.In a Limited Liability Company (LLC), how are profits and losses typically distributed among members?

a) Equally b) Based on the number of members

c) In proportion to their ownership percentage d) Based on investment amounts

48.What is the tax rate for C Corporations on taxable income over $50,000 but not over $75,000?

a) 22% b) 24% c) 21% d) 20%

49. A business entity that fails to pay its payroll taxes on time may be subject to:
a) A late filing penalty. b) A trust fund recovery penalty.
c) An accuracy-related penalty. d) A failure-to-file penalty.

50. Which entity offers limited liability protection to its owners and allows them to avoid double taxation?
a) Limited Liability Company (LLC) b) Partnership
c) C Corporation d) Sole Proprietorship

51. If a partnership does not file its tax return, which penalty might apply?
a) $100 per month per partner b) 10% of the total tax liability
c) $1,000 per month d) 5% of the total tax liability

52. The primary purpose of Form SS-4 is to apply for:
a) A business license
b) A sales tax permit
c) An Employer Identification Number (EIN)
d) Workers' Compensation Insurance

53. Business meal expenses are deductible in 2024 at what percentage, provided they are ordinary and necessary business expenses?
a) 50% b) 75% c) 100% d) Not deductible

54. The Work Opportunity Tax Credit (WOTC) is available to employers who hire individuals from certain:
a) Geographic locations b) Industry sectors
c) Targeted groups d) Educational backgrounds

55. Which of the following best describes a business's "basis" in property?
a) The property's fair market value at the time of purchase
b) The cost of the property plus any improvements minus depreciation
c) Only the amount financed through debt
d) The assessed value for property tax purposes

56. The tax year for a C Corporation:
a) Must align with the calendar year.
b) Can be a fiscal year that is different from the calendar year.
c) Is determined by the IRS and cannot be changed.
d) Must match the tax year of its shareholders.

57. A business entity that offers liability protection to its owners but is taxed on its income at the entity level is a:
a) Sole Proprietorship
b) Partnership
c) C Corporation
d) S Corporation

58. When a partnership liquidates, the distribution of assets to the partners is generally:
a) Taxed as ordinary income to the partners.
b) Considered a tax-free return of capital to the extent of the partner's basis in the partnership.
c) Subject to self-employment tax.
d) Treated as dividend income.

59. A key characteristic of an S Corporation is that:
a) It pays income tax at the corporate level
b) Its income and losses are passed through to shareholders
c) It can have an unlimited number of shareholders
d) Its shareholders must be non-resident aliens

60. The Accumulated Earnings Tax is designed to:
a) Penalize C Corporations for not distributing dividends
b) Encourage S Corporations to convert to C Corporations
c) Tax partnerships on retained earnings
d) Prevent businesses from retaining excess earnings to avoid paying dividends to shareholders

Part II - Section 2: Business Financial Information

1.Which financial statement shows a company's revenues and expenses over a specific period?

a) Balance sheet b) Statement of cash flows

c) Income statement d) Statement of retained earnings

2.What does EBITDA stand for in financial terms?

a) Earnings Before Income Tax Deductions and Amortization

b) Earnings Before Interest, Taxes, Depreciation, and Amortization

c) Earnings Before Income Taxes, Depreciation, and Amortization

d) Earnings Before Interest, Taxes, Dividends, and Amortization

3.The quick ratio assesses a company's ability to cover its short-term liabilities with:

a) Cash and equivalents

b) Cash, accounts receivable, and inventory

c) Cash, marketable securities, and inventory

d) Cash, accounts receivable, and marketable securities

4.Which financial ratio measures a company's ability to pay off its short-term liabilities with its most liquid assets?

a) Debt-to-Equity Ratio b) Current Ratio c) Quick Ratio d) Return on Assets

5.The DuPont analysis breaks down return on equity (ROE) into three components: net profit margin, asset turnover and:

a) Debt-to-Equity Ratio b) Total Assets c) Return on Investment d) Equity Multiplier

6.What financial metric evaluates the efficiency of a company's inventory management?

a) Inventory Turnover Ratio b) Accounts Receivable Turnover

c) Debt Ratio d) Return on Assets

7.A high debt-to-equity ratio generally indicates:
a) Better financial health b) Lower risk for creditors
c) Higher financial leverage d) Greater liquidity

8.Which financial statement shows a company's assets, liabilities, and shareholders' equity at a specific point in time?
a) Balance sheet b) Income statement
c) Statement of cash flows d) Statement of retained earnings

9. Which of the following entities can elect to be treated as an S Corporation?
a) Sole Proprietorship b) C Corporation c) Partnership d) Trust

10.The debt ratio is calculated by dividing a company's total liabilities by its:
a) Total Assets b) Shareholders' Equity c) Net Income d) Retained Earnings

11.Which financial metric measures the efficiency of a company in collecting its accounts receivable?
a) Accounts Receivable Turnover Ratio b) Inventory Turnover Ratio
c) Debt Ratio d) Quick Ratio

12.A high return on assets (ROA) signifies:
a) Inefficient use of assets b) Higher profitability relative to its asset base
c) Lower debt d) A decline in market share

13.What does the term "EBT" stand for in financial terms?
a) Earnings Before Taxes b) Earnings Before Total Expenses
c) Earnings Before Interest and Taxes d) Earnings Before Income and Taxes

14.The equity multiplier is calculated by dividing a company's total assets by its:
a) Total Liabilities
b) Shareholders' Equity
c) Retained Earnings
d) Earnings Before Interest and Taxes

15.Which financial ratio measures a company's ability to cover its interest expenses with its earnings before interest and taxes (EBIT)?
a) Debt Ratio b) Interest Coverage Ratio
c) Return on Equity d) Gross Profit Margin

16. For tax purposes, which form is used to report the sale or exchange of assets by a business?
a) Form 4797 b) Form 4562 c) Form 8824 d) Schedule D

17. Employer contributions to qualified retirement plans are:
a) Not deductible as a business expense
b) Deductible up to 25% of compensation paid
c) Fully deductible as a business expense
d) Considered taxable income to the employee

18.Which of the following represents the formula for Return on Assets (ROA)?
a) Net Income / Average Total Assets
b) Net Income / Shareholders' Equity
c) Total Assets / Net Income
d) Shareholders' Equity / Total Assets

19.A higher Debt-to-Equity Ratio generally indicates:
a) Lower financial risk b) Lower leverage
c) Higher financial risk d) A balanced financial structure

20. The deduction for business meals in 2024 is limited to what percentage of the expense?
a) 50% b) 60% c) 70% d) 100%

21.Which financial ratio measures a company's ability to generate earnings before interest and taxes on total assets?
a) Return on Assets (ROA) b) Earnings Per Share (EPS)
c) Asset Turnover Ratio d) Return on Equity (ROE)

22. Which of the following statements about the Qualified Business Income Deduction is correct?

a) It is available to C Corporations.

b) It allows a deduction of up to 50% of qualified business income.

c) It is available to businesses regardless of the taxpayer's total taxable income.

d) It applies to income from sole proprietorships, S corporations, partnerships, and LLCs.

23.A corporation's payment of dividends to shareholders is:

a Deductible as a business expense b) Treated as a distribution from earnings and profits
c) Subject to self-employment tax d) Reported on Schedule K-1

24.A higher Inventory Turnover Ratio generally implies:

a) Efficient inventory management b) Slow inventory turnover
c) Lower sales volume d) Decreased liquidity

25. A calendar-year corporation must file its income tax return (Form 1120) by:

a) March 15 b) April 15 c) May 15 d) July 15

26.Return on Equity (ROE) is calculated as:

a) Net Income / Average Total Assets

b) Net Income / Shareholders' Equity

c) Total Assets / Net Income

d) Shareholders' Equity / Total Assets

27.Which ratio measures a company's ability to pay off short-term liabilities with its most liquid assets excluding inventory?

a) Acid-Test Ratio b) Asset Turnover Ratio
c) Debt-to-Equity Ratio d) Earnings Per Share (EPS)

28.A higher Price-to-Earnings (P/E) ratio typically indicates:

a) Lower growth prospects b) Higher expected earnings growth
c) Lower market confidence d) Higher risk exposure

29.The DuPont Analysis decomposes Return on Equity (ROE) into which two key components?

a) Asset Turnover and Profit Margin

b) Debt Ratio and Interest Coverage

c) Earnings Before Taxes and Earnings After Taxes

d) Inventory Turnover and Accounts Receivable Turnover

30. Which of the following qualifies for a 100% bonus depreciation?

a) Used property acquired in a trade

b) Certain new and used property placed in service after September 27, 2017

c) Buildings

d) Intangible assets

31.The depreciation method that allows for an immediate expense deduction rather than capitalizing and depreciating over time is:

a) Straight-line depreciation b) MACRS c) Section 179 d) Bonus depreciation

32.The Debt-to-Equity ratio measures:

a) Liquidity b) Profitability c) Financial leverage d) Asset management

33.Form 1120S is filed by:

a) C Corporations b) S Corporations c) Partnerships d) Limited Liability Companies

34.The Current Ratio is calculated by dividing:

a) Current assets by current liabilities b) Total assets by total liabilities

c) Net income by total assets d) Cash by inventory

35.The Return on Equity (ROE) measures:

a) A company's ability to generate profit from its shareholders' investment

b) The efficiency of inventory management

c) The liquidity of a company

d) The net income of a company

36.Inventory Turnover Ratio is calculated by dividing:

a) Cost of goods sold by average inventory b) Sales by average inventory

c) Net income by average inventory d) Accounts receivable by inventory

37.The Gross Profit Margin is calculated by dividing:

a) Net sales by net income b) Cost of goods sold by net sales

c) Gross profit by net sales d) Gross profit by total revenue

38.Which of the following is considered a deductible business expense?

a) Political contributions b) Expenses associated with illegal activities

c) Charitable contributions d) Personal expenses

39.The Debt Ratio is calculated by dividing:

a) Total liabilities by total assets b) Total assets by total equity

c) Net income by total assets d) Cash by current liabilities

40.The due date for a calendar-year partnership tax return (Form 1065) is:

a) March 15 b) April 15 c) May 15 d) June 15

41.The Cash Ratio measures:

a) The liquidity of a company b) The solvency of a company

c) The profitability of a company d) The efficiency of a company

42. The form used by an employer to report an employee's annual wages and taxes withheld is:

a) Form W-2 b) Form W-4 c) Form 1099-NEC d) Form 1040

43.The Operating Cash Flow Ratio is calculated by dividing:

a) Operating cash flow by net income

b) Operating cash flow by current liabilities

c) Operating cash flow by total assets

d) Operating cash flow by total liabilities

44. The business use of home deduction requires which IRS form for reporting?

a) Schedule C b) Form 8829 c) Form 2106 d) Schedule A

45.The Efficiency Ratio is concerned with:

a) How efficiently a company uses its assets

b) How effectively a company manages its liabilities

c) How much profit a company generates

d) How fast a company grows its sales revenue

46.What does Return on Assets (ROA) measure?

a) Profit margin b) Liquidity c) Efficiency in using assets d) Debt-to-Equity ratio

47.A business can carry forward a Net Operating Loss (NOL) for:

a) 5 years b) 10 years c) 20 years d) Indefinitely

48.Which statement best defines Gross Profit Margin?

a) The ratio of gross profit to total revenue

b) The ratio of net income to total revenue

c) The ratio of operating income to net sales

d) The ratio of operating expenses to net sales

49.What is the Debt-to-Equity Ratio used for?

a) To assess the company's liquidity

b) To evaluate the company's profitability

c) To measure the company's financial leverage

d) To determine the company's inventory turnover

50.What does the Accounts Receivable Turnover Ratio measure?

a) The time it takes to pay off debt

b) The efficiency in collecting cash from customers

c) The ability to pay short-term debt

d) The liquidity of a company's assets

51. Which financial ratio assesses the proportion of assets financed by debt?
a) Debt ratio b) Quick ratio c) Current ratio d) Inventory turnover ratio

52. What is the purpose of the Operating Cash Flow Ratio?
a) To measure the company's efficiency in using its assets to generate cash flow
b) To assess the company's liquidity position
c) To evaluate the company's financial leverage
d) To calculate the company's debt service coverage

53. What is the Inventory Turnover Ratio used to evaluate?
a) How effectively a company manages its inventory
b) The company's return on investment
c) The company's ability to cover short-term debt
d) The company's operating efficiency

54. What does the Quick Ratio primarily focus on?
a) Inventory turnover b) Cash and near-cash assets to cover current liabilities
c) Long-term solvency d) Profitability

55. The annual depreciation deduction for a passenger automobile used 100% for business in the first year of service cannot exceed (for 2023):
a) $10,000 b) $20,200 c) $25,000 d) $1,000,000

56. What does the Asset Turnover Ratio measure?
a) The efficiency of using assets to generate sales
b) The company's ability to cover short-term debt
c) The company's liquidity position d) The company's return on investment

57. Payroll taxes reported on Form 941 include:
a) Only federal income tax withholdings
b) Federal income tax withholdings and FUTA tax
c) Federal income tax withholdings, Social Security, and Medicare taxes
d) Only FUTA tax

58.What does the Price-Earnings (P/E) Ratio measure?

a) The number of shares issued by a company

b) The market price of a stock relative to its earnings per share

c) The company's return on investment

d) The company's debt-to-equity ratio

59.What financial ratio evaluates the percentage of profit a company retains after covering all expenses?

a) Debt ratio

b) Profit Margin

c) Times Interest Earned ratio

d) Inventory turnover ratio

60.Which financial ratio measures the efficiency of a company's cash management?

a) Current ratio

b) Quick ratio

c) Cash Conversion Cycle

d) Debt-to-Equity ratio

Part II - Section 3: Specialized Returns and Taxpayers

1. Taxpayers report transactions involving virtual currency on:
a) Form 8949 b) Schedule D c) Form 1099-K d) Both A and B

2.A C corporation's tax year generally ends on the last day of which month?
a) January b) February c) March d) December

3. Tax-exempt interest income is reported on which line of Form 1040?
a) Line 2a b) Line 8b c) Line 21 d) Line 24

4. The Heavy Highway Vehicle Use Tax is reported annually on:
a) Form 2290 b) Form 720 c) Form 1120 d) Schedule F

5. A U.S. citizen living abroad files Form 1116 to:
a) Report foreign-earned income. b) Claim foreign tax credit.
c) Disclose foreign bank accounts. d) Exclude housing costs.

6.In a Limited Liability Company (LLC), how are profits typically allocated among members?
a) Equally b) Based on the number of members
c) Based on the initial investment d) As specified in the operating agreement

7. A disqualified person engaging in an excess benefit transaction with a tax-exempt organization must report the transaction on:
a) Form 4720 b) Form 990 c) Form 1040 d) Schedule K-1

8. The purpose of Form 8886 is to disclose:
a) Foreign bank and financial accounts.
b) Reportable transaction understatement.
c) Interest in foreign trusts.
d) Gifts from foreign persons.

9. Schedule K-1 is used in reporting a partner's share of income in:

a) A corporation. b) A trust. c) A partnership. d) An S corporation.

10. Form 5329 is filed for:

a) Additional taxes on IRAs and other tax-favored accounts.

b) Reporting agricultural taxes.

c) Claiming energy credits.

d) Reporting non-cash charitable contributions.

11. The tax form for an S Corporation to elect S status is:

a) Form 2553 b) Form 1120S c) Form 8832 d) Schedule K-1

12. What is the primary purpose of Form 1120S?

a) Reporting income from partnerships

b) Reporting income from C corporations

c) Reporting income from S corporations

d) Reporting income from sole proprietorships

13. Which tax form is used to report income from a charitable trust?

a) Form 1120 b) Form 1041 c) Form 1065 d) Form 990

14. Form 8879 is the IRS e-file signature authorization form for:

a) Estates and trusts. b) Corporations. c) Individuals. d) Partnerships.

15. An individual participating in a high deductible health plan (HDHP) may contribute to a Health Savings Account (HSA) and report contributions on:

a) Form 8889 b) Form 1099-SA c) Form 5498-SA d) Schedule C

16. The form used by an exempt organization to request a change in the accounting period is:

a) Form 1128 b) Form 990 c) Form 8822 d) Form 1023

17. Excise taxes paid on fuel are reported using:

a) Form 4136 b) Form 2290 c) Form 720 d) Form 8849

18.In which form would a partnership report the distributions made to its partners?

a) Schedule K-1 (Form 1065) b) Form 1120 c) Form 1065 d) Form 1040

19. The form filed by a business to report a change in accounting method is:

a) Form 3115 b) Form 2106 c) Form 1120 d) Form 8822

20.What is the tax form used to report income from a foreign corporation with U.S. shareholders?

a) Form 1065 b) Form 1120 c) Form 5471 d) Form 8804

21.When is the tax return for a partnership due if it operates on a fiscal year ending on June 30?

a) September 15 b) October 15 c) November 15 d) December 15

22. Form 3468 is used to claim:

a) The investment credit. b) The earned income credit.

c) The foreign tax credit. d) The child and dependent care credit.

23. The International Fuel Tax Agreement (IFTA) return for reporting fuel taxes by interstate motor carriers is filed through:

a) The state's taxation department.

b) Form 720.

c) Form 2290.

d) Form 8849.

24. To report information on a tax shelter, a taxpayer would use Form:

a) 8886

b) 8271

c) 8697

d) 4720

25. A tax-exempt organization's unrelated business income tax return is filed on:

a) Form 990 b) Form 990-EZ c) Form 990-T d) Form 1023

26. Form 8300 is filed to report:

a) Cash payments over $10,000 received in a trade or business.

b) Transactions involving virtual currency.

c) Foreign bank and financial account holdings.

d) Large gifts received from foreign entities.

27.Which form is used to report income from a partnership with foreign partners?

a) Form 1065 b) Form 1120 c) Form 5471 d) Form 8804

28.The Form 5500 is required for:

A. Reporting foreign bank accounts. B. Employee benefit plan reporting.

C. Non-profit organizations' annual reporting. D. Corporate income tax reporting.

29.Which tax form is used to report income from foreign financial accounts?

a) Form 1120 b) Form 1040 c) Schedule B (Form 1040) d) Form 8938

30.What is the maximum contribution limit for a Roth IRA in 2023 for individuals under 50 years old?

a) $5,000 b) $5,500 c) $6,000 d) $6,500

31.Form 720 is used to report:

A. Quarterly Federal Excise Taxes.

B. Annual information returns for tax-exempt organizations.

C. Income and deductions for partnerships.

D. U.S. income tax for estates and trusts.

32.What is the maximum age limit for a child to qualify for the Child and Dependent Care Credit?

a) 12 years old b) 13 years old c) 17 years old d) 18 years old

33. Which form is used by farmers to report farm income and expenses?

a) Schedule F b) Schedule C c) Form 1120 d) Form 4835

34. The tax form used by a non-profit organization to report its annual financial information is:

a) Form 990 b) Form 1065 c) Form 1120 d) Schedule K-1

35. Which form is used to report gambling winnings?

a) Form W-2G b) Schedule C c) Form 5754 d) Schedule A

36.What is the maximum income threshold for claiming the Lifetime Learning Credit in 2023?

a) $55,000 b) $60,000 c) $65,000 d) $90,000

37.Non-profit organizations claim tax-exempt status by filing:

a) Form 1023 b) Form 1040 c) Form 1065 d) Form 1120S

38.A farmer electing to average their income over three years would use which schedule with Form 1040?

a) Schedule F

b) Schedule J

c) Schedule A

d) Schedule SE

39. Estates and trusts report income on:

a) Form 1041 b) Form 706 c) Form 709 d) Form 1040

40.What is the maximum annual contribution limit for a Coverdell Education Savings Account (ESA)?

a) $1,000

b) $2,000

c) $3,000

d) $4,000

41.Under what condition can a taxpayer use Form 1041?
a) Reporting income from rental real estate
b) Reporting income from a trust or estate
c) Reporting income from a partnership
d) Reporting income from a corporation

42. The Tax Cuts and Jobs Act impacted the alimony payments made under divorce or separation agreements executed after December 31, 2018, by:
a) Making them non-deductible by the payer and non-taxable to the recipient
b) Increasing the deduction for the payer
c) Making them fully taxable to the payer
d) None of the above

43.What is the fling status for a taxpayer whose spouse passed away in the previous tax year and has a dependent child?
a) Single b) Head of household
c) Married fling separately d) Qualifying widow(er) with dependent child

44. For the Adoption Credit, qualified adoption expenses are reported on:
a) Form 8839 b) Form 8863 c) Schedule 3 (Form 1040) d) Form 1040, Line 12a

45. Which form do taxpayers use to claim the credit for the elderly or the disabled?
a) Form 1040 Schedule R b) Form 8862 c) Form 2441 d) Schedule 3 (Form 1040)

46. A taxpayer selling their primary residence must report the sale on:
a) Form 8949 b) Schedule D
c) Both A and B d) No need to report if capital gains are below the exclusion amount

47. The Kiddie Tax applies to:
a) The unearned income of children under the age of 18
b) The earned income of children under the age of 18
c) Both earned and unearned income of children under the age of 18
d) The unearned income of children under age 19, or full-time students under age 24

48.Form 990-T is used by tax-exempt organizations to report:

a) Charitable contributions.

b) Unrelated business taxable income.

c) Foreign bank and financial accounts.

d) Farming income.

49. The form used by military reservists, qualified performing artists, and fee-basis government officials to deduct unreimbursed employee business expenses is:

a) Form 2106

b) Schedule C

c) Form 1040 Schedule 1

d) These expenses are no longer deductible

50.When is the tax return for a partnership due if it operates on a fiscal year ending on September 30?

a) December 15 b) January 15 c) February 15 d) March 15

51.Which tax form is used to report income from a Real Estate Mortgage Investment Conduit (REMIC)?

a) Form 1065 b) Form 1120 c) Form 1066 d) Form 1040

52.What is the maximum contribution limit for a Health Savings Account (HSA) in 2023 for individuals under 50 years old?

a) $3,000 b) $3,500 c) $3,850 d) $4,000

53.In which form would a shareholder report income received from a Real Estate Investment Trust (REIT)?

a) Form 1065 b) Form 1120 c) Form 1120-REIT d) Form 1040

54.What tax form is used to report income from a Foreign Sales Corporation (FSC)?

a) Form 1120 b) Form 1120-FSC c) Form 5471 d) Form 8804

55. A minister's housing allowance is:
a) Taxable for federal income tax purposes but exempt from self-employment tax
b) Exempt from both federal income tax and self-employment tax
c) Exempt from federal income tax but subject to self-employment tax
d) Taxable for both federal income tax and self-employment tax

56.The tax form used by a political organization to report taxable income is:
a) Form 1120-POL b) Form 8871 c) Form 8872 d) Form 990

57.When is the deadline for fling a Form 990 for tax-exempt organizations with a fiscal year ending on December 31?
a) April 15 b) May 15 c) June 15 d) July 15

58. Taxpayers with net investment income and modified adjusted gross income above certain thresholds may be subject to:
a) Additional Medicare Tax
b) Net Investment Income Tax (NIIT)
c) Alternative Minimum Tax (AMT)
d) Both A and B

59.To claim a tax credit for research and experimental expenditures, a business files:
a) Form 6765
b) Form 8826
c) Form 3800
d) Schedule C

60. Who must file Form 709, United States Gift (and Generation-Skipping Transfer) Tax Return?
a) Any taxpayer receiving a gift
b) Taxpayers whose gifts to any one individual exceed the annual exclusion amount
c) Taxpayers making gifts that do not exceed the lifetime exemption
d) Only taxpayers gifting real estate

PART 2

BUSINESSES

Fill in the Blank Questions

Part 2: Businesses
Fill in the blank questions

1. The maximum Section 179 expense deduction for businesses in 2023 is __________.

2. Since 2023, the filing threshold for the electronic filing of Forms 1099 was __________ or more forms.

3. The due date for calendar year corporations to file Form 1120 in 2024 is __________.

4. The 2023 tax rate for corporations on income over $10 million is __________ percent.

5. For 2023, the maximum contribution limit per employee under a SEP plan is __________ or __________ percent of compensation, whichever is less.

6. The penalty for a business failing to file Form 1099-NEC when required is up to __________ per form.

7. Businesses can claim a credit for increasing research activities, commonly known as the R&D credit, which is __________ percent of qualified expenses.

8. The maximum number of employees a business can have to be eligible for the Small Business Health Care Tax Credit in 2023 is __________.

9. A business that purchases a new electric vehicle for business use in 2023 can claim a maximum federal tax credit of up to __________.

10. The limit on the deduction for meals and entertainment expenses provided to employees and necessary for business operations in 2023 is __________ percent.

11. The depreciation method required under MACRS for most new non-residential real property placed in service after 1986 is the __________ method.

12. The maximum deduction allowed under the Qualified Business Income (QBI) Deduction for 2023 is __________ of qualified business income.

13. The threshold for a business to be required to use the accrual method of accounting, based on average annual gross receipts for the preceding three years, is more than __________.

14. A corporation can deduct charitable contributions up to __________ percent of its taxable income.

15. For 2023, the credit for employer-provided child care facilities and services is limited to __________ of the expenses incurred.

16. The penalty for not making required minimum distributions (RMDs) from a company's defined benefit plan is __________ of the amount that should have been distributed.

17. A business can carry forward Net Operating Losses (NOLs) incurred in 2023 to future tax years indefinitely, but the deduction in any future year is limited to __________ percent of taxable income.

18. The maximum credit for small employer pension plan startup costs is __________ of the cost to set up and administer the plan and educate employees about the plan, up to a maximum of __________ per year for the first three years.

19. The maximum amount a business can invest in equipment and property and still qualify for the full Section 179 deduction in 2023 is __________.

20. For tax year 2023, a business entity that is classified as a large partnership must have more than __________ partners.

21. The due date for businesses to provide Forms W-2 to their employees for the 2023 tax year is __________.

22. The standard cost recovery period under MACRS for office furniture is _________ years.

23. The percentage of health insurance premiums that small businesses can claim as a credit under the Small Business Health Care Tax Credit for 2023 is up to __________ percent.

24. The maximum foreign-derived intangible income (FDII) deduction for corporations in 2023 is __________ percent of FDII.

25. The excise tax on the investment income of private foundations for 2023 is ______ percent.

26. Before 2023, the filing threshold for the electronic filing of Forms 1099 was __________ or more forms.

27. For 2023, the payroll tax credit for increasing research activities for qualified small businesses is capped at __________.

28. The luxury auto depreciation cap for a passenger vehicle placed in service in 2023 is __________ for the first year.

29. A C corporation can deduct dividends received from another taxable domestic corporation at a rate of up to __________ percent, depending on ownership percentage.

30. The cap on the deduction for business interest expense in 2023 is limited to __________ percent of adjusted taxable income.

31. Bonus Depreciation was allowed at __________ percent for all qualified purchases made between September 27, 2017, and January 1, 2023.

32. For 2023, the percentage of net earnings from self-employment subject to the self-employment tax is __________ percent.

33. For 2024, Bonus Depreciation will be reduced to _______ percent for qualified property.

34. The maximum age at which a designated beneficiary can inherit an IRA or retirement plan account and stretch distributions over their own life expectancy is __________.

35. The maximum amount of start-up expenditures a business can elect to deduct in the first year of operation in 2023 is __________.

36. The threshold for the application of the uniform capitalization rules to producers of real or tangible personal property in 2024 is annual gross receipts of more than ___________ over the last three years.

37. The maximum penalty for a corporation's failure to disclose a reportable transaction on Form 8886 is ___________.

38. The depreciation recovery period for residential rental property under MACRS is ___________ years.

39. The due date for filing IRS Form 5500 for a plan year ending on December 31, 2023, is ___________.

40. The number of days within which a business must generally deposit FUTA (Federal Unemployment Tax Act) taxes is ___________ days after the end of the quarter in which the liability arose.

41. The maximum Section 199A Qualified Business Income Deduction for a qualifying joint filer in 2023 is ___________ percent of combined qualified business income.

42. The bonus depreciation percentage for qualified property placed in service in 2023 is ___________ percent.

3. The threshold for the application of the uniform capitalization rules to producers of real or tangible personal property in 2023 is annual gross receipts of more than ___________ over the last three years.

44. The recovery period under MACRS for new farming equipment and machinery is ___________ years.

45. The maximum contribution to a defined benefit plan in 2024 is ___________ or ___________ percent of the participant's average compensation for his or her highest three consecutive calendar years, whichever is less.

46. The amount of compensation over which the additional Medicare tax applies for a single filer in 2023 is__________.

47. The total annual sales volume at which a retail or wholesale business is required to use the accrual method of accounting is __________.

48. The maximum contribution to a defined benefit plan in 2023 is__________ or __________ percent of the participant's average compensation for his or her highest three consecutive calendar years, whichever is less.

49. For the tax year 2023, the due date for partnerships and S corporations to file Schedule K-1 with the IRS is __________.

50. The total per diem rate for travel to a high-cost locality, before subtracting the portion treated as paid for meals according to § 274(n), is $_________.

51. For travel to any other locality within CONUS, the portion of the $214 low rate treated as paid for meals for purposes of § 274(n) is $_________.

52. The excise tax rate on high-cost employer-sponsored health coverage, also known as the "Cadillac tax," for 2023 is __________ percent (note: this tax has been repeatedly delayed).

53. The maximum allowable net passive income for an S corporation before it incurs a tax penalty is __________ percent of gross receipts.

54. The percentage deduction allowed for Domestic Production Activities (DPA) before it was repealed was __________ percent.

55. For 2023, the specific identification method of inventory costing requires that the actual physical flow of goods be __________ to the cost flow.

56. The tax credit available to small businesses for the costs of conducting accessibility improvements for the disabled in 2023 is up to __________ percent of expenditures over $250, not to exceed __________.

57. The daily per diem rate for meals and incidental expenses for high-cost localities in the continental United States in 2023 under the high-low method is __________.

58. The maximum depreciation deduction for passenger automobiles placed in service in 2023 and not subject to bonus depreciation is __________ in the first year.

59. The threshold at which a partnership is required to remit taxes using the Electronic Federal Tax Payment System (EFTPS) in 2023 is __________.

60. The new markets tax credit, aimed at investments in certain low-income communities, provides a credit over seven years totaling __________ percent of the original investment amount.

61. The maximum amount a business can claim for the Work Opportunity Tax Credit per qualifying veteran employee in 2023 is __________.

62. The deductible portion of self-employed health insurance premiums in 2023 is __________ percent.

63. The filing fee for the IRS application for recognition of exemption under section 501(c)(3) is __________ if gross receipts are expected to average not more than $10,000 annually over a four-year period.

64. The deduction for business entertainment expenses directly related to the active conduct of a trade or business before 2023 was __________ percent.

65. The simplified dollar-value LIFO inventory method threshold for eligibility in 2023 is __________ in average annual gross receipts for the three preceding years.

66. The penalty for late payment of payroll taxes is __________ percent of the unpaid taxes for each month or part of a month the payment is late, up to a maximum of __________ percent.

67. The maximum deduction under IRC Section 179D for energy-efficient commercial building property placed in service in 2023 is __________ per square foot.

68. In 2023, the threshold for gross receipts that triggers the requirement for C corporations to use the accrual method of accounting is __________.

69. The deduction for business entertainment expenses directly related to the active conduct of a trade or business in 2023 is __________ percent.

70. The limit on the number of participants for a business to be considered for the simplified employee pension (SEP) plan is __________.

71. Businesses must capitalize and amortize most section 197 intangibles over __________ years.

72. The 2023 depreciation limit for luxury automobiles for the second year in service, not subject to bonus depreciation, is __________.

73. The maximum amount of Orphan Drug Credit a company can claim in 2023 is __________ percent of qualified clinical testing expenses.

74. To revoke a Subchapter S election made on Form 2553, the revocation statement must be received by the IRS by the requested effective date unless it's for the first day of the tax year, in which case it is due by the 16th day of the __________ month of the tax year.

75. The maximum penalty for a partnership's failure to provide a correct Schedule K-1 to a partner is __________ per K-1.

76. If an S corporation on a December 31 tax year ending requests a revocation effective February 14, the statement of revocation must be submitted to the IRS no later than __________.

77. An applicable corporation, as defined for the purposes of CAMT, must calculate its CAMT liability using Form __________ as per section 55 of the Internal Revenue Code starting in tax years after __________.

78. The maximum amount that can be contributed to a health savings account (HSA) by an individual with self-only coverage in 2023 is __________.

79. The due date for quarterly estimated tax payments for corporations for Q4 of the 2023 tax year is __________.

80. What is the maximum credit amount a taxpayer can receive for a qualified 2-wheeled plug-in electric vehicle under Internal Revenue Code Section 30D(g)?

81. The maximum dollar limit for contributions to an employee's defined contribution plan in 2023 is __________.

82. The recovery period under MACRS for qualified improvement property placed in service in 2023 is __________ years.

83. The limit on annual contributions to a Simple IRA for an employee aged 50 or over in 2023 is __________.

84. The threshold for the annual tax on net investment income of private colleges and universities per student in 2023 is __________.

85. The percentage of compensation a business can claim as a credit for paid family and medical leave in 2023 is up to __________ percent.

86. The maximum carryback period for a Net Operating Loss (NOL) occurring in the tax year 2023 is __________ years.

87. The threshold amount for the deduction of certain business start-up and organizational expenses in 2023 before the phase-out begins is __________.

88. The maximum penalty for failing to file Form 5472 (Information Return of a 25% Foreign-Owned U.S. Corporation or a Foreign Corporation Engaged in a U.S. Trade or Business) per form per month, up to a maximum of __________ months, is __________.

89. The bonus depreciation rate for certain qualified improvement property placed in service in 2024 is __________ percent.

90. The deduction for business meals provided by a restaurant before 2023 was __________ percent of the expense.

91. The maximum percentage of income a Qualified Small Business can exclude from CGS taxation for qualified small business stock sold after being held for more than 5 years is __________ percent.

92. The inflation adjustment factor for determining the limitation on the deduction for luxury passenger automobiles in 2023 is __________.

93. The maximum duration for which the Empowerment Zone Employment Credit can be claimed for each qualified employee is __________ years.

94. The maximum amount of wages and tips eligible for the credit for employer-paid Social Security and Medicare taxes on employee tips in 2023 is __________.

95. The first-year bonus depreciation percentage for qualified business use property acquired and placed in service in 2023 is __________ percent.

96. The annual limit for elective deferrals to a 401(k) plan by employees under the age of 50 in 2023 is __________.

97. Form __________ is used by S Corporations to report income, deductions, and credits to the IRS.

98. The business structure that provides owners with limited liability protection but is treated as a pass-through entity for tax purposes is a(n) __________.

99. Businesses must file Form __________ to report payments made to independent contractors if they pay $600 or more during the tax year.

100. Form __________ is utilized by employers to report federal unemployment taxes.

101. A __________ is the portion of payroll taxes withheld from employees' wages by the employer and paid directly to the government.

102. The depreciation system used for tax purposes that allows for faster depreciation in the early years of an asset's life is known as __________.

103. Businesses use Form __________ to claim a tax credit for research and development expenses.

104. The __________ method of accounting records income when it is received and expenses when they are paid.

105. __________ taxes are taxes imposed on employers based on the salaries and wages paid to employees.

106. An Employer Identification Number (EIN) is required for businesses and can be obtained by filing Form __________ with the IRS.

107. Form __________ is used by taxpayers to request a change in their accounting period.

108. Businesses must file Form __________ to report social security and Medicare taxes withheld from employees' wages and the employer's portion of these taxes.

109. The deduction for business meals provided by a restaurant in 2023 is __________ percent of the expense.

110. The bonus depreciation rate for certain qualified improvement property placed in service in 2025 is __________ percent.

111. What is the percentage of the cost of any qualified 2-wheeled plug-in electric vehicle that can be credited according to Internal Revenue Code Section 30D(g) for the taxable year?

112. The maximum dollar limit for contributions to an employee's defined contribution plan in 2024 is __________.

113. The annual limit for elective deferrals to a 401(k) plan by employees under the age of 50 in 2024 is __________.

114. The 2023 depreciation limit for luxury automobiles for the third year in service is __________.

PART 3

REPRESENTATION

Multiple-Choice Questions

Part III - Section 1: Practices and Procedures

1.What is the statute of limitations for the IRS to assess additional tax on a filedreturn without substantial omissions?

a) 1 year b) 2 years c) 3 years d) 4 years

2.Under Circular 230, what is the deadline for maintaining records of tax returns and other documents for Enrolled Agents?

a) 2 years b) 3 years c) 4 years d) 5 years

3.Which of the following is not a prohibited practice for Enrolled Agents according to Circular 230?

a) Negligence b) Failure to sign tax returns

c) Charging an unconscionable fee d) Taxpayer representation before a Revenue Officer

4.Which form is used to authorize a tax professional to represent a taxpayer before the IRS?

a) Form 8821 b) Form 2848 c) Form 4506 d) Form 9465

5.What is the IRS Electronic Filing Identification Number (EFIN) used for?

a) Filing tax returns electronically b) Authorizing representation

c) Validating dependent information d) Requesting penalty abatement

6.Which entity may appeal a decision in a Collection Due Process (CDP) hearing?

a) Sole proprietor b) Trustee c) LLC member d) Taxpayer

7. To request a Collection Due Process hearing with the IRS, a taxpayer must file Form:

a) 12153 b) 9465 c) 433-F d) 2848

8.In which situation can an Enrolled Agent disclose taxpayer information without consent?

a) To a tax practitioner b) During an IRS audit

c) When fling a tax return d) None of the above

9.What is the IRS form used to request an extension of time to file a tax return?

a) Form 1040 b) Form 4868 c) Form 1099 d) Form W-2

10.What is the first step in the process of offering a compromise on tax liabilities with the IRS?

a) Complete Form 656 b) Payment submission c) Taxpayer interview d) Financial analysis

11. The Centralized Authorization File (CAF) number is used to:

a) Track a taxpayer's balance due

b) Identify a tax professional authorized to access taxpayer information

c) Record a taxpayer's installment agreement details

d) File a tax return electronically

12.What is the primary purpose of the Taxpayer Advocate Service (TAS)?

a) To enforce tax laws b) To represent taxpayers in court

c) To assist taxpayers facing hardships d) To audit taxpayer records

13. The IRS Office of Appeals is independent of the IRS's:

a) Commissioner's office

b) Examination and Collection functions

c) Legal department

d) All of the above

14.When does the IRS generally issue refunds for electronically filed tax returns? a) 4 weeks b) 6 weeks c) 8 weeks d) 10 weeks

15.Which of the following is not a requirement to become an Enrolled Agent?

a) Passing the Special Enrollment Examination (SEE)

b) Prior work experience with the IRS

c) Satisfactory background check

d) Maintaining Continuing Education credits annually

16.What's the primary role of Circular 230 in tax practice?
a) Mandates tax rates b) Defines tax liability
c) Governs practice before the IRS d) Dictates tax exemptions

17.When is a Taxpayer Information Authorization (Form 8821) typically used?
a) To represent a taxpayer in court b) To request a refund from the IRS
c) To authorize disclosure of information to third parties d) To file joint returns

18. Form 843 is used to request:
a) An installment agreement b) A tax court petition
c) An abatement of tax-related penalties d) Power of attorney

19. What is the consequence under Circular 230 for an enrolled agent who willfully misrepresents a client's tax liabilities?
a) Suspension b) Monetary fine c) Disbarment d) All of the above

20.In the context of tax practices, what does AICPA stand for?
a) American Institute of Certified Public Accountants b) Association of Internal Certified Public Accountants c) Agency for Internal Certified Public Audits d) American Institute of Certified Professional Advisors

21.What is a tax practitioner required to do to e-filetax returns?
a) Obtain a PTIN b) Complete Form 4868 c) Obtain a TIN d) Complete Form 8821

22. The Fresh Start initiative helps taxpayers by:
a) Offering free tax preparation services
b) Providing expanded access to installment agreements and Offers in Compromise
c) Automatically waiving late payment penalties
d) Expediting refunds

23.What does the acronym EIN stand for in tax practice?
a) Estimated Income Number b) Employer Identification Number
c) Exemption Inclusion Notice d) External Income Nexus

24.Which IRS form is used to apply for an installment agreement?

A. Form 9465 B. Form 2848 C. Form 433-A D. Form 8821

25.The Taxpayer Bill of Rights includes how many fundamental rights?

a) 5 b) 8 c) 10 d) 12

26.When is a Power of Attorney required in tax practice?

a) To obtain a PTIN b) To represent a taxpayer before the IRS

c) To file an extension d) To request a refund

27.Which organization sets ethical standards for tax professionals?

a) AICPA b) IRS c) FASB d) SEC

28. The Trust Fund Recovery Penalty is applied to:

a) Every employee of a business with unpaid payroll taxes

b) The business entity itself for failure to pay employment taxes

c) Responsible individuals who willfully fail to collect or pay employment taxes

d) Any vendor providing services to the business

29.What is the penalty for failure to furnish a copy of a tax return or refund information?

a) $50 b) $200 c) $500 d) $2,000

30.In accordance with Circular 230, when must an enrolled agent disclose a conflict of interest to a client?

a) Immediately upon discovery b) Within 10 days of discovery

c) Before engaging in representation d) After obtaining consent to continue representation

31.What does a Taxpayer Information Authorization (Form 8821) typically allow?

a) Access to tax return information

b) Representation before the IRS

c) Authorization to disclose information to third parties

d) Request for tax transcripts

32. The Preparer Tax Identification Number (PTIN) is required for:

a) All taxpayers

b) IRS employees who prepare tax returns

c) Professionals who prepare tax returns for compensation

d) Taxpayers filing their own tax return electronically

33.A request for innocent spouse relief must be made using Form:

a) 8857 b) 8379 c) 1040X d) 8822

34.The IRS provides an automated underreporter notice, also known as:

a) CP2000 b) CP501 c) CP503 d) CP504

35.An Offer in Compromise is submitted using Form:

a) 656

b) 433-A (OIC)

c) Both A and B

d) 8821

36.What does Circular 230 primarily address?

a) Tax deduction guidelines

b) Taxpayer exemptions

c) Ethical and practice standards for tax professionals

d) IRS penalty computation

37.Which organization regulates enrolled agents?

a) AICPA b) IRS c) FASB d) SEC

38.What information does an ERO (Electronic Return Originator) primarily provide in tax practice?

a) Tax preparation services

b) Digital tax return fling services

c) IRS audit representation

d) Tax exemption guidelines

39.What's the purpose of Form 8879 in tax practice?

a) Authorize representation before the IRS b) Electronically sign a tax return

c) Request an extension d) Report tax liabilities

40.What does a Preparer Tax Identification Number (PTIN) enable a tax professional to do?

a) Access taxpayer information b) File tax returns on behalf of clients

c) Represent clients in court d) Obtain an EFIN

41.What is the duration within which the IRS generally processes e-filed tax returns?

a) Within 24 hours b) Within 48 hours c) Within 72 hours d) Within 21 days

42.What's the role of the IRS Office of Professional Responsibility?

a) Enforce tax rates b) Regulate tax deductions

c) Oversee the ethical conduct of tax professionals d) Process tax refunds

43.What is the penalty for failing to file a tax return without reasonable cause?

a) 5% of the tax due per month b) $500 c) $1,000 d) 50% of the tax due

44.Circular 230 governs the practice of:

a) All taxpayers

b) IRS employees

c) Tax professionals authorized to represent taxpayers before the IRS

d) State tax authorities

45.What is the purpose of Form 8822 in tax practice?

a) File an extension

b) Notify the IRS of change of address

c) Request a refund

d) Amend a tax return

Section 2: Representation before the IRS

1. An offer in compromise allows a taxpayer to:

a) Delay tax payments without penalty

b) Settle their tax debt for less than the full amount owed

c) Avoid an audit

d) Appeal an IRS decision without going to court

2.When might a taxpayer need to file Form 2848?

a) To file a joint return b) To authorize disclosure to third parties

c) To request a refund d) To claim dependents

3. The collection statute expiration date (CSED) for a tax debt is generally:

a) 5 years from the assessment date b) 10 years from the assessment date

c) 15 years from the filing date d) 20 years from the filing date

4.In tax representation matters, what does "POA" stand for?

a) Power of Association b) Power of Attorney

c) Practitioner of Authority d) Public Office Authorization

5. Taxpayers have the right to be informed, which includes the right to:

a) Know the maximum time they have to challenge the IRS's position

b) Know the maximum amount of time the IRS has to audit or collect a tax debt

c) Be provided clear explanations of the law and IRS procedures in all tax forms, instructions, publications, notices, and correspondence

d) All of the above

6. Form 656 is used for:

a) Requesting a tax court trial

b) An offer in compromise

c) Filing an appeal with the IRS Office of Appeals

d) Authorizing a third party to receive confidential tax information

7.In the context of representation before the IRS, what does "EA" stand for?

a) Enrolled Accountant b) Enrolled Attorney

c) Enrolled Agent d) Exempted Advocate

8. The Fresh Start program is designed to:

a) Provide tax credits to first-time homebuyers

b) Help taxpayers with overdue taxes by offering flexible payment options

c) Offer free tax preparation services

d) Educate young taxpayers about their tax responsibilities

9.An enrolled agent must renew their PTIN:

a) Every year b) Every three years

c) Only once; it does not expire d) Every five years

10. A taxpayer who disagrees with the IRS's proposed changes to their tax return has the right to:

a) Only discuss the changes with the auditor

b) Accept the changes without appeal

c) Request a conference with the auditor's manager

d) Appeal to the U.S. Supreme Court directly

11.Which of the following is NOT a requirement for becoming an enrolled agent?

a) Passing the Special Enrollment Examination b) Holding a current PTIN

c) Completing a degree in accounting d) Undergoing a tax compliance check

12. Enrolled agents are subject to which of the following requirements?

a) Mandatory retirement age of 65

b) Continuing education requirements

c) A minimum number of tax returns prepared each year

d) Residency requirements in the United States

13. Which form is filed by an individual or entity to report a change of address?

a) Form 8822 b) Form 8821 c) Form 2848 d) Form 433-A

14.The right to finality means a taxpayer has the right to:

a) Know the maximum amount of time they have to challenge the IRS's position

b) Expect the IRS to finalize an audit within a year

c) Know that the IRS has a limited time to audit a tax year or collect a tax debt

d) All of the above

15. The right to retain representation when dealing with the IRS is established under:

a) The Taxpayer Bill of Rights b) Circular 230

c) The Internal Revenue Code d) The U.S. Constitution

16. The primary purpose of Form 911, Request for Taxpayer Advocate Service Assistance, is to:

a) Report IRS employee misconduct

b) Request an extension to file

c) Seek help resolving tax problems that haven't been resolved through normal channels

d) Notify the IRS of identity theft

17. How long must an enrolled agent retain authorization forms from clients for the direct deposit of tax refunds?

a) 2 years b) 4 years

c) 5 years d) 6 years

18. The Office of Professional Responsibility (OPR) oversees the conduct of:

a) All taxpayers

b) IRS employees only

c) Tax professionals authorized to practice before the IRS

d) State tax agencies

19.When is a Circular 230 disclosure required to be included in written communications with taxpayers?

a) Only in the case of tax liabilities over $10,000

b) If the communication is over three pages long

c) If the written communication is furnished to a client regarding tax advice

d) If requested by the taxpayer

20.What is the penalty amount for failing to comply with Circular 230 requirements?
a) $1,000 b) $2,500 c) $5,000 d) $10,000

21.An enrolled agent is representing a taxpayer in an IRS audit. During the process, the IRS requests documentation. What should the enrolled agent do?
a) Provide only the documents the IRS specifically requests
b) Provide all relevant documents to facilitate the audit
c) Request the IRS to clarify the documentation needed
d) Decline to provide any documents until the audit is completed

22.Under Circular 230, what is the primary goal for an enrolled agent representing a client before the IRS?
a) Ensure a reduction in tax liabilities b) Achieve the best outcome for the taxpayer
c) Comply with all IRS directives and regulations d) Protect the integrity of the tax system

23.In a representation case, if an enrolled agent discovers errors in a taxpayer's prior tax flings, what is the best course of action?
a) Immediately report the errors to the IRS
b) Ignore the errors to avoid complications
c) Correct the errors and discuss options with the taxpayer
d) Inform the taxpayer to rectify the errors independently

24. The Practitioner Priority Service (PPS) is:
a) A hotline for taxpayers to report unethical tax preparers
b) A dedicated phone service for tax professionals to obtain assistance with client issues
c) A program for high-priority processing of amended returns
d) An expedited service for tax refund inquiries

25.When can an enrolled agent disclose taxpayer information to third parties under Circular 230?
a) Only with the taxpayer's written consent b) When it benefits the enrolled agent financially
c) If it assists in resolving an audit d) When requested by the IRS

26.When representing a taxpayer, an enrolled agent cannot:

a) Charge a contingent fee for services related to an IRS audit

b) Disclose taxpayer information to third parties without written consent

c) Appeal an IRS decision

d) Request a taxpayer's record of account from the IRS

27.What action should an enrolled agent take if they receive a notice of suspension from practice before the IRS?

a) Continue representing clients until the suspension is enforced

b) Notify all clients immediately and cease representation

c) Appeal the suspension within 30 days

d) Ignore the notice until further instructions are received

28.The Taxpayer Advocate Service (TAS) is:

a) A division of the Department of Justice

b) An independent organization within the IRS

c) Part of the U.S. Tax Court

d) A private sector nonprofit organization

29.What is the primary purpose of the due diligence requirements under Circular 230 for enrolled agents?

a) To reduce potential penalties for taxpayers

b) To ensure accurate and complete tax flings

c) To speed up the tax return process

d) To facilitate quicker refunds for clients

30.During an IRS audit, if an enrolled agent encounters conflicts of interest between clients, what should be the enrolled agent's approach?

a) Represent the client who paid a higher fee

b) Cease representation for both clients

c) Work impartially to resolve conflicts

d) Represent the client with the most significant tax liabilities

31. Circular 230 Section 10.51 lists conduct subject to disciplinary action, which does NOT include:
a) Failing to file a personal tax return
b) Failing to provide a copy of a tax return to a client
c) Conviction of any criminal offense under the revenue laws of the United States
d) Soliciting business by promising results that cannot be guaranteed

32.What action should a tax professional take if they are unable to meet a client's expectations regarding representation?
a) Immediately terminate the relationship
b) Engage in deceptive practices to meet expectations
c) Communicate clearly and manage client expectations realistically
d) Submit an appeal to the IRS on behalf of the client

33.Circular 230 governs:
a) Only CPAs and attorneys
b) All tax preparers
c) Individuals authorized to practice before the IRS
d) IRS employees

34.When does Circular 230 require tax practitioners to stop representing a taxpayer?
a) When the representation becomes complex
b) When the taxpayer doesn't pay the representation fees
c) When the tax issue is resolved
d) When the taxpayer's interests are adverse to the practitioner's

35.In which scenario is it essential to obtain the taxpayer's consent before representing them before the IRS?
a) When the IRS requests immediate representation
b) When the taxpayer's spouse is involved in the issue
c) When the taxpayer's attorney is unavailable
d) When the taxpayer is represented by a tax-exempt organization

36.What's the maximum penalty a tax practitioner could face for violating Circular 230?

a) $500

b) $1,000

c) $2,000

d) There is no monetary penalty specified

37.What action should a tax professional take if they discover an error in a client's tax return during representation?

a) Hide the error from the IRS

b) Notify the IRS immediately

c) Correct the error and inform the client about the necessary steps

d) Continue representation without addressing the error

38.When is it permissible for a tax practitioner to withdraw representation from a client?

a) When the tax practitioner funds the client uncooperative

b) When the IRS escalates the case

c) When the tax practitioner disagrees with the taxpayer's opinion

d) When the taxpayer doesn't pay the representation fees

39.What is the primary objective of Circular 230 in terms of representation before the IRS?

a) To impose limitations on taxpayer representation

b) To ensure taxpayers avoid representation before the IRS

c) To establish guidelines for practitioners' conduct in representing taxpayers

d) To regulate the fees charged by tax practitioners

40.What's the primary responsibility of an Enrolled Agent when representing a taxpayer before the IRS?

a) To ensure the taxpayer gets the maximum refund possible

b) To negotiate the lowest possible tax liability for the taxpayer

c) To ensure compliance with tax laws while advocating for the taxpayer's rights

d) To prioritize the taxpayer's interests over tax regulations

41.Under what circumstances might a tax practitioner not need to obtain a power of attorney (Form 2848) to represent a taxpayer before the IRS?
a) When representing a minor child b) When the taxpayer is represented by an attorney c) When the tax issue is straightforward d) When the taxpayer requests anonymity

42.What is the key role of Publication 947 in tax representation?
a) Provides guidelines for completing tax forms
b) Outlines penalties for tax evasion
c) Offers guidance for tax professionals representing taxpayers before the IRS
d) Details IRS regulations for charitable donations

43.How does Circular 230 define due diligence concerning tax representation?
a) Obtaining maximum tax refunds for clients
b) Conducting a comprehensive background check on clients
c) Exercising thoroughness and accuracy in preparing and advising on tax matters
d) Establishing a quick resolution for tax disputes

44.In which situation might a tax practitioner be required to terminate representation before the IRS?
a) When the IRS extends the statute of limitations
b) When the taxpayer's income increases
c) When the taxpayer becomes bankrupt
d) When the representation becomes unreasonably difficult or impracticable

45.What does Circular 230 stipulate regarding conflicts of interest in tax representation?
a) Tax practitioners must always favor the IRS's position over the taxpayer's interests
b) Tax practitioners can't represent a taxpayer if they previously represented the IRS on the same matter
c) Tax practitioners must prioritize their financial interests over the taxpayer's concerns
d) Tax practitioners must disclose conflicts of interest to the taxpayer and proceed if the taxpayer agrees

Part III - Section 3: Specific Types of Representation

1. Taxpayers who cannot fully pay their taxes may apply for which program to settle for less than the full amount owed?
a) Offer in Compromise b) Installment Agreement
c) Currently Not Collectible status d) Penalty Abatement

2. In what situation might a tax professional use Form 2848 on behalf of a client?
a) To report annual income b) To grant power of attorney for IRS representation
c) To request a tax extension d) To file an amended tax return

3. Which statement best describes the purpose of Form 12203?
a) Request for an Installment Agreement
b) Appeal to the Office of Appeals
c) Authorization for a third-party designee
d) Power of attorney for state tax representation

4. When would a taxpayer likely use Form 843?
a) To claim a refund or abatement of taxes, penalties, and interest
b) To apply for an extension to file taxes
c) To request a payment plan from the IRS
d) To amend a previous tax return

5. What does the Collection Due Process (CDP) hearing allow for taxpayers?
a) The opportunity to appeal the denial of an Offer in Compromise
b) An opportunity to claim additional deductions
c) A chance to extend the tax payment deadline
d) The ability to request an audit

6. Which form should be used to request an Offer in Compromise?
a) Form 656 b) Form 8821 c) Form 12203 d) Form 2848

7.In what circumstances might a taxpayer use Form 911?

a) To report a tax preparer for unethical practices

b) To request a payment plan from the IRS

c) To apply for an Offer in Compromise

d) To request assistance during a significant financial hardship

8.What does the acronym CNC stand for in IRS representation?

a) Currently Not Collectible b) Collection Notice Control

c) Creditor Negotiation Contract d) Collection Negotiation Clause

9.What is the primary function of Form 911 in IRS representation?

a) Request for a taxpayer advocate

b) Application for a tax extension

c) Power of attorney for state tax representation

d) Authorization to disclose tax information

10.In which situation might a taxpayer request innocent spouse relief?

a) When they are audited for a tax year filed jointly with a spouse

b) If they believe their spouse or former spouse should be solely responsible for a tax bill

c) When they want to separate their tax liabilities from their spouse

d) All of the above

11. Which IRS form is used to appeal a decision regarding the Trust Fund Recovery Penalty?

a) Form 12153 b) Form 843 c) Form 656 d) Form 2751

12.In what situation would a taxpayer most likely use Form 9465?

a) To report foreign assets b) To claim additional deductions

c) To request an extension to file taxes d) To apply for a payment plan

13.What is the purpose of Form 13844?

a) To request an Installment Agreement b) To apply for an Offer in Compromise

c) To report foreign income d) To request a Collection Due Process hearing

14.What does the acronym OIC stand for in the context of IRS representation?

a) Offer in Contract b) Offer in Circumstance c) Offer in Compromise d) Offer in Claim

15.In what scenario would a taxpayer use Form 12153?

a) To request a payment plan b) To report a tax preparer for unethical practices

c) To request a Collection Due Process hearing d) To authorize disclosure of tax information

16.What is the form used to request innocent spouse relief?

a) Form 8379 b) Form 8857 c) Form 2848 d) Form 9465

17. Enrolled agents are authorized to represent taxpayers in:

a) Preparing and filing tax returns only

b) Matters before the IRS, but not in Tax Court

c) All matters including Tax Court if they pass the Tax Court Practitioner Exam

d) Appeals and Collections matters only

18. Innocent spouse relief is requested to:

a) Separate a taxpayer's liability from that of their spouse or ex-spouse.

b) Correct a mistake made by a spouse on a joint return.

c) Claim a refund that was applied to the spouse's past debt.

d) Remove penalties applied due to a spouse's actions.

19.When might a taxpayer seek a Collection Alternative?

a) To expedite tax refunds b) To increase tax liabilities

c) To provide more time to pay tax debts d) To avoid IRS correspondence

20.Which form do taxpayers use to request a reduction or removal of penalties?

a) Form 843

b) Form 9465

c) Form 1040X

d) Form 2848

21.Under what condition would a taxpayer file Form 843?

a) To claim a refund of interest and penalties

b) To appeal an audit determination

c) To request an Offer in Compromise

d) To initiate a Collection Due Process hearing

22. The IRS may issue a Notice of Deficiency, also known as a "90-day letter," which gives the taxpayer:

a) 90 days to file a past-due return.

b) 90 days to pay the assessed tax.

c) 90 days to petition the Tax Court without paying the disputed amount.

d) 90 days to request an administrative appeal.

23.Which form is specifically designed for taxpayers to dispute an employment tax adjustment or determination?

a) Form 1120 b) Form 941-X c) Form 843 d) Form 1040X

24.What does Form 433-A involve?

a) Requesting Currently Not Collectible status

b) Requesting an Installment Agreement

c) Providing financial information for a Collection Alternative

d) Requesting a Collection Due Process hearing

25. The __________ is used to determine a taxpayer's ability to pay an outstanding tax liability.

a) Form 433-A (OIC) b) Form 433-F c) Form 9465 d) Form 656

26.Taxpayers involved in bankruptcy proceedings should know that taxes:

A. Are always discharged in bankruptcy

B. May be discharged, depending on the type of tax and timing of the bankruptcy

C. Can never be discharged in bankruptcy

D. Are only dischargeable in Chapter 11 bankruptcies

27. Circular 230 addresses:
a) The rights of taxpayers
b) The conduct of IRS agents
c) The practices of tax professionals authorized to represent taxpayers
d) Federal tax law only

28. When might a taxpayer seek Currently Not Collectible status?
a) To accelerate tax payments b) To reduce tax liabilities
c) To temporarily suspend IRS collection actions d) To avoid tax audits

29. A __________ hearing provides taxpayers an opportunity to discuss lien or levy actions taken by the IRS.
a) Collection Due Process (CDP)
b) Collection Appeal Program (CAP)
c) Trust Fund Recovery Penalty (TFRP)
d) Unified Audit Procedure (UAP)

30. The IRS program designed to help resolve large, complex business tax issues before tax returns are filed is called:
a) Fast Track Settlement b) Pre-filing Agreement Program
c) Offers in Compromise d) Advanced Pricing Agreement

31. Which program offers low-income taxpayers free representation in tax disputes?
a) Volunteer Income Tax Assistance (VITA)
b) Tax Counseling for the Elderly (TCE)
c) Low-Income Taxpayer Clinics (LITCs)
d) Annual Filing Season Program (AFSP)

32. Representation before the IRS does NOT include:
a) Communicating with the IRS on behalf of a taxpayer
b) Preparing a taxpayer's return
c) Providing legal advice on tax matters
d) Negotiating with the IRS for an installment agreement

33.When might a taxpayer file Form 12153?

a) To request an Installment Agreement

b) To request innocent spouse relief

c) To appeal a rejected Offer in Compromise

d) To request a Collection Due Process hearing

34. To represent a taxpayer in a tax court, an enrolled agent must:

a) Pass a special tax court exam.

b) Be also licensed as an attorney.

c) Have a CPA certification.

d) Simply have an active PTIN.

35.Which IRS division handles large and international business tax issues?

a) Small Business/Self-Employed Division b) Wage and Investment Division

c) Large Business and International Division

d) Tax Exempt and Government Entities Division

36.What does Form 656 facilitate?

a) To claim a refund of interest and penalties

b) To request an Installment Agreement

c) To settle tax debts for less than the full amount

d) To provide financial information for a Collection Alternative

37.Representation in the U.S. Tax Court, without the need for a legal degree, is permitted for:

a) All CPAs b) Enrolled agents who pass the Tax Court's examination

c) Any taxpayer representing themselves d) Family members of the taxpayer

38.An enrolled agent who wants to participate in the Annual Filing Season Program must:

A. Pass a comprehensive tax law exam every year

B. Complete a specific number of continuing education hours annually

C. Be licensed by their state's board of accountancy

D. Submit a new application to the IRS each year

39. Which of the following is a reason for a taxpayer to file Form 8857, Request for Innocent Spouse Relief?

a) They wish to change their filing status from joint to single

b) They were unaware of their spouse's understatement of tax

c) They have unfiled tax returns for past years

d) They disagree with the IRS over a tax deduction

40. The Trust Fund Recovery Penalty applies to:

a) Any taxpayer who owes back taxes

b) Business owners responsible for unpaid employment taxes

c) Individuals who fail to report offshore bank accounts

d) Taxpayers who underreport their income

41. What form does a taxpayer typically use to appeal an IRS decision to levy their property? a) Form 9465 b) Form 12153 c) Form 12153 d) Form 433-F

42. Which IRS form is used to request an audit reconsideration?

a) Form 12153 b) Form 843 c) Form 886-H d) Form 4549

43. When might a taxpayer file Form 12203?

a) To request an audit reconsideration b) To appeal a rejected Installment Agreement

c) To request an Offer in Compromise d) To request a Collection Due Process hearing

44. What's the primary purpose of Form 843?

a) To request an Installment Agreement b) To claim a refund of taxes, interest, or penalties

c) To appeal an IRS decision on a rejected Offer in Compromise

d) To request innocent spouse relief

45. In what situation might a taxpayer use Form 911?

a) To request an Installment Agreement

b) To appeal an IRS decision on a rejected Offer in Compromise

c) To request Taxpayer Advocate Service assistance

d) To settle tax debts for less than the full amount

Part III - Section 4: Completion of the Filing Process

1. Form 433-F, Collection Information Statement, is used to:
a) File an appeal with the IRS Office of Appeals b) Request a collection due process hearing
c) Provide financial information to the IRS to set up a payment plan or compromise d) Update the taxpayer's filing status.

2. An Offer in Compromise is submitted to the IRS to:
a) Contest an IRS audit finding b) Request a reduction of assessed penalties and interest
c) Propose a settlement for less than the full amount of taxes owed d) Apply for a tax lien release.

3. When is the last date for a taxpayer to file an extension for their individual tax return? a) March 15 b) April 15 c) September 15 d) October 15

4. The Protecting Americans from Tax Hikes (PATH) Act affects refunds by:
a) Delaying refunds for taxpayers claiming the Earned Income Tax Credit (EITC) or Additional Child Tax Credit (ACTC) until February 15 b) Increasing the speed of refund processing for all taxpayers c) Requiring additional documentation for all refunds over $2,000 d) Automatically auditing returns claiming EITC or ACTC

5. Which document must be filed with the IRS to initiate an appeal of an IRS decision?
a) A written protest b) Form 1040X
c) Form 12203, Request for Appeals Review d) A letter of intent

6. The purpose of Form 12277 is:
a) To apply for an installment agreement b) To request withdrawal of a filed Notice of Federal Tax Lien c) To appeal a decision made by the IRS Office of Appeals
d) To designate a taxpayer's representative

7. Form 56 is used to:
a) Notify the IRS of the creation or termination of a fiduciary relationship.
b) Apply for an Employer Identification Number (EIN) c) Report noncash charitable contributions d) Request a copy of a previously filed tax return.

8. Which IRS tool allows taxpayers to view their tax account transactions and statements?
a) Direct Pay b) IRS2Go app c) Online Account d) EFTPS

9. To temporarily stop collection activity due to financial hardship, a taxpayer would request: a) An Offer in Compromise b) Currently Not Collectible status
c) A streamlined installment agreement d) An extension to pay

10. What's the deadline for providing employees with their W-2 forms?
a) January 15 b) February 15 c) March 15 d) April 15

11. Which form is used to report interest income that is more than $1,500?
a) Form 1099 b) Form W-2 c) Schedule B (Form 1040) d) Form 1040

12. What's the tax form used by self-employed individuals to compute and pay their quarterly estimated taxes? a) Form 1040 b) Form 1099 c) Form 1040-ES d) Form W-2

13. What is the form used to report real estate transactions?
a) Form 1040 b) Form 1099 c) Schedule A (Form 1040) d) Form 1098

14. Form 1040-ES is used for:
a) Amending an individual tax return b) Making estimated tax payments for individuals
c) Reporting self-employment income d) Claiming the foreign-earned income exclusion

15. An extension of time to pay the tax owed can be requested with Form:
a) 9465 b) 1127 c) 4868 d) 1040X

16. What is the purpose of Form 1099-MISC?
a) Reporting wages and salaries b) Reporting interest and dividends
c) Reporting miscellaneous income d) Reporting capital gains

17. Form 1099-MISC is issued to: a) Employees for wages earned b) Independent contractors for non-employee compensation c) Banks for interest paid on savings accounts
d) Corporations for dividends paid to shareholders

18.The Electronic Federal Tax Payment System (EFTPS) is used for:

a) Filing electronic tax returns b) Paying federal taxes online or by phone

c) Requesting tax return transcripts d) Authorizing a representative to speak to the IRS

19. The maximum amount of time the IRS generally has to charge additional tax or audit a tax return is known as the:

a) Refund statute expiration date b) Tax return due date

c) Collection statute expiration date d) Assessment statute expiration date

20. Which form is used to request a copy of a tax return directly from the IRS?

a) Form 4506 b) Form 4506-T c) Form 8822 d) Form 2848

21. Which of the following is NOT a method for making federal tax payments?

a) EFTPS b) Direct Pay c) PayPal d) Credit or debit card

22.What is the primary purpose of Form 8962?

a) Reporting education expenses b) Claiming the Earned Income Credit

c) Calculating Premium Tax Credit d) Reporting retirement contributions

23.What is the penalty for not having health insurance (individual mandate) as per the Affordable Care Act?

a) $200 b) 2.5% of household income above the tax return fling threshold

c)$695 per adult d) $0 starting from the tax year 2019.

24.An automatic extension of time to file a U.S. individual income tax return is requested with Form:

a) 4868 b) 8822 c) 7004 d) 8868

25. The IRS issues __________ to taxpayers as confirmation that their electronic tax return has been accepted).

a) An audit letter b) A notice of deficiency

c) An acknowledgment letter d) A balance due notice

26. Taxpayers who wish to disclose a previously unreported offshore financial account must file:

a) Form 8938 b) FinCEN Form 114, FBAR c) Form 1040 Schedule B d) Form 2555

27. To participate in the IRS Annual Filing Season Program, tax preparers must complete:

a) 18 hours of continuing education including a six-hour federal tax law update course.

b) 72 hours of continuing education every three years.

c) A comprehensive tax law exam administered by the IRS annually.

d) An ethics exam every year.

28. If a taxpayer discovers they made a mistake on their original tax return, they should:

a) Wait for the IRS to find the mistake and issue a correction.

b) File an amended return immediately to correct the mistake.

c) Ignore the mistake if it results in a refund)

d) Pay additional tax owed with the next year's return.

29.Which IRS publication provides detailed information about the IRS collection process?

a) Publication 1 b) Publication 15 c) Publication 594 d) Publication 946

30.What is the fling status for a taxpayer who is unmarried and doesn't qualify for any other fling status?

a) Single b) Head of household

c) Married fling separately d) Qualifying widow(er) with dependent child

31.What is the purpose of Form 4868?

a) Request for an Offer in Compromise

b) Application for Automatic Extension of Time to File U.S. Individual Income Tax Return

c) Authorization for tax representation d) Request for Innocent Spouse Relief

32.What is the purpose of Form 8822, Change of Address?

a) To notify the IRS of a change in tax return preparer b) To request a change in tax filing status c) To inform the IRS of a taxpayer's new address d) To update a taxpayer's bank account information for direct deposit

33. The electronic filing (e-file) system for tax returns:

a) Is optional for all taxpayers
b) Requires special software or a tax professional
c) Can only be used if the taxpayer owes taxes
d) Is not available for amended tax returns.

34. Which form should a taxpayer use to report capital gains and losses?

a) Schedule A (Form 1040)
b) Form 8949
c) Form 1099-MISC
d) Form 4684

35. What is the penalty for failing to file a tax return?

a) 10% of the tax due
b) 5% of the tax due per month, up to 25%
c) $100
d) No penalty

36. If a taxpayer disagrees with an IRS determination, they can appeal to the:

a) Taxpayer Advocate Service
b) U.S. District Court
c) Office of Appeals
d) State Tax Commission

37. What is the penalty for underpayment of estimated tax by an individual taxpayer?

a) 2% of the underpayment amount
b) 10% of the underpayment amount
c) 1% of the underpayment amount
d) No penalty for underpayment

38. Taxpayers who are victims of identity theft should:

a) File a police report and notify the IRS immediately.
b) Wait for the IRS to notify them of potential fraud)
c) Pay any fraudulent tax liabilities to avoid penalties.
d) Change their Social Security number.

39. Form 9465 is used to request:

a) An installment agreement for paying taxes owed.
b) An extension of time to file.
c) Innocent spouse relief.
d) Correction of an SSN on a tax return.

40. The IRS issues most refunds within:

a) 21 days of e-filing b) 60 days of e-filing.

c) 90 days of paper filing d) 6 months of filing, regardless of the method)

41. Direct Deposit is:

a) The only way to receive a tax refund

b) An option that can speed up refund processing.

c) Not available for tax refunds.

d) Slower than receiving a paper check.

42. An IRS levy can be released if the taxpayer:

a) Agrees to pay the full amount owed within 30 days.

b) Proves that the levy is causing an economic hardship.

c) Files an amended return.

d) Appeals the levy without proposing a payment plan.

43.A taxpayer can check the status of their refund using:

a) The Where's My Refund? tool on the IRS website.

b) Form 8821, Tax Information Authorization.

c) Calling the IRS's toll-free number and providing their SSN.

d) All of the above.

44. A taxpayer who doesn't have a bank account can receive their refund via:

a) Direct deposit to a friend's account b) A paper check

c) IRS credit, applicable to next year's taxes d) Cash pick-up at an IRS office

45. What does a CP2000 notice from the IRS indicate?

a) An audit is being initiated.

b) There is a proposed change based on a mismatch between income reported by the taxpayer and information returns.

c) The taxpayer's refund is being held.

d) The taxpayer has underpaid estimated tax payments.

PART 3

REPRESENTATION

Fill-in-the-Blank Questions

Part 3: Representation
Fill in the blank questions

1. A taxpayer must file Form 2848, Power of Attorney and Declaration of Representative, to authorize an individual to represent them before the IRS. The representation rights for Enrolled Agents are __________ to those of attorneys and CPAs.

2. The __________ Rule requires practitioners to provide competent representation to their clients.

3. Practitioners are prohibited from __________ by the IRS Standards of Practice, which includes the preparation of a tax return based on information that the practitioner knows or should know is incorrect.

4. The annual renewal period for PTINs (Preparer Tax Identification Numbers) begins in __________.

5. The IRS may impose a __________ penalty on preparers who engage in conduct subject to penalty under section 6694.

6. A taxpayer has __________ years from the date of payment to claim a refund if no tax return was filed.

7. The __________ provides taxpayers with the right to pay no more than the correct amount of tax.

8. Taxpayers have the right to challenge the IRS's position and be heard, known as the __________.

9. Circular 230 governs practice before the IRS and applies to all __________ who represent taxpayers before the IRS.

10. The IRS Office of Professional Responsibility (OPR) enforces standards of practice for tax professionals such as attorneys, CPAs, and __________.

11. An offer in compromise allows taxpayers to settle their tax debt for less than the full amount owed if they can prove __________ or __________.

12. The IRS Fresh Start initiative makes it easier for taxpayers to __________ and __________ tax liens.

13. Under the Taxpayer Bill of Rights, every taxpayer has the right to __________ representation.

14. The __________ Act is a key piece of legislation that outlines the powers and responsibilities of the IRS.

15. The taxpayer's right to finality means they have the right to know the maximum time they have to challenge the IRS's position and the maximum time the IRS has to __________ a tax return.

16. A tax return preparer is primarily responsible for the tax return's accuracy regarding __________ claims and information provided by the taxpayer.

17. If a taxpayer disagrees with an IRS decision, they can appeal to the __________.

18. The IRS must always inform taxpayers about the __________ of any collection actions against them.

19. Practitioners must adhere to the principle of __________, ensuring that their conduct does not discredit the profession.

20. The __________ can issue injunctions against tax return preparers who engage in fraudulent or deceptive practices.

21. To protect taxpayers' rights, the IRS established the __________ in 1996.

22. The maximum amount the IRS can charge for a taxpayer to make an installment agreement as of 2023 is __________.

23. The __________ is responsible for helping taxpayers resolve problems with the IRS and for advocating on their behalf.

24. When the IRS proposes a change to a tax return, it sends the taxpayer a(n) __________ explaining the proposed changes.

25. A __________ summons is a tool the IRS uses to compel a taxpayer or third party to provide information or documents.

26. An Enrolled Agent must complete a minimum of __________ hours of continuing education per year, including __________ hours on ethics.

27. An Enrolled Agent must complete __________ hours of continuing education every three years.

28. Practitioners are prohibited from endorsing or otherwise negotiating any __________ issued to a client.

29. Taxpayers have the right to be informed, which includes the right to know what they need to do to __________ under the law.

30. The principle of confidentiality under Circular 230 means a practitioner cannot disclose any __________ of the client without the client's permission.

31. A __________ is an agreement between a taxpayer and the IRS where the taxpayer agrees to pay off their tax debt within a certain period.

32. The __________ provides independent oversight of the IRS and reports to Congress.

33. The Collection Due Process (CDP) hearing gives taxpayers the opportunity to appeal the IRS's decision before __________ is taken against their property.

34. The __________ doctrine allows the IRS to disallow tax benefits under transactions that don't have substantial economic effects aside from their tax benefits.

35. Under the Privacy Act of 1974, taxpayers have the right to request their IRS records via a(n) __________ request.

36. The __________ allows taxpayers to sue the government for wrongful collection actions.

37. Taxpayers have the right to confidentiality, which means unauthorized disclosure of their tax information by an IRS employee could result in a __________ penalty against the employee.

38. The __________ limits the time within which the IRS must collect outstanding taxes to 10 years from the date of assessment.

39. Taxpayers can make an __________ disclosure to the IRS to potentially avoid criminal charges for tax evasion by voluntarily reporting previously undisclosed income.

40. A __________ is a formal written statement to the IRS disputing a proposed adjustment or collection action.

41. The Taxpayer Bill of Rights was established to ensure that taxpayers have a fundamental understanding of their rights within the __________.

42. An __________ conference is a pre-appeal meeting offered to taxpayers as an opportunity to settle a dispute before formal appeal.

43. Tax practitioners must avoid conflicts of interest or obtain a __________ from all affected clients.

44. Circular 230 outlines the duties and restrictions relating to __________, including the use of electronic media to provide tax advice.

45. The __________ act requires tax return preparers to obtain and use a Preparer Tax Identification Number (PTIN).

46. If a taxpayer does not agree with the IRS over a tax matter, they can request a hearing with the __________.

47. To represent a taxpayer in front of the IRS, one must not be _______ under Circular 230.

48. The __________ privilege allows a taxpayer to refuse to disclose certain confidential communications with a federally authorized tax practitioner to the IRS.

49. Practitioners are required to exercise __________ when practicing before the IRS, meaning they must not negligently or intentionally disregard the rules.

50. The maximum amount of time the IRS grants for an automatic extension to file individual income tax returns is __________ months.

51. Taxpayers can appeal certain IRS decisions within the IRS prior to litigation in __________ court.

52. The __________ Credit is an incentive for low-income taxpayers to save for retirement, which they can claim on their tax return.

53. The __________ decision-making process allows a taxpayer to understand how the IRS made its decision.

54. Taxpayers can request an abatement of penalties if they can show __________ cause for failure to comply with tax laws.

55. __________ is the term for the illegal practice of preparing tax returns with the intent to commit fraud or evasion.

56. The IRS uses the __________ program to identify potentially fraudulent returns filed by identity thieves.

57. Under Circular 230, a practitioner must not engage in __________ for the purpose of delaying or impeding tax administration.

58. The __________ ensures taxpayers are informed about IRS decisions regarding their tax account and receive clear explanations of the outcomes.

59. A taxpayer's written consent is required for a tax practitioner to __________ their tax return information.

60. The __________ provides guidelines for determining a taxpayer's ability to pay outstanding tax liabilities.

61. Taxpayers who receive a(n) __________ from the IRS have 90 days to petition the Tax Court.

62. The __________ is an IRS tool for taxpayers to check the status of their amended return.

63. __________ occurs when the IRS applies a taxpayer's refund to a tax debt from a prior year.

64. The IRS maintains a __________ that lists individuals who are barred from practicing before the IRS.

65. The __________ provides a summary of the taxpayer's tax liability and payments for the year.

66. The annual program for qualifying non-resident aliens to resolve tax issues is known as the __________ Program.

67. A __________ is required for a tax practitioner to discuss a client's tax matters with the IRS over the phone.

68. The __________ is an agreement between the United States and other countries to exchange tax information in order to combat tax evasion.

69. The right to a fair and just tax system is one of the ten rights in the __________.

70. The __________ allows a taxpayer to represent themselves or to have a representative in dealings with the IRS.

71. The IRS must provide a(n) __________ to the taxpayer if it intends to contact third parties during an examination.

72. Tax practitioners must not unreasonably delay the prompt __________ of any matter before the IRS.

73. A taxpayer can grant specific authorization for a representative to receive and inspect confidential tax information via Form __________.

74. Taxpayers have the right to retain an __________ copy of their signed tax return.

75. The IRS may issue a(n) __________ to employers who repeatedly fail to deposit employment taxes as required.

76. Under the First Time Abate policy, the IRS may abate the __________ for taxpayers who have not previously been required to file or have no prior penalties for the preceding three tax years.

77. If a taxpayer's offer in compromise is rejected, they have __________ days to appeal the decision.

78. A(n) __________ is an informal review process for taxpayers who disagree with an IRS determination.

79. A practitioner may charge a(n) __________ fee, which must be based on the actual work performed and not contingent on the outcome of the tax matter.

80. Taxpayers have the right to make audio recordings of their meetings with the IRS, provided they give __________ days advance notice.

81. A(n) __________ agreement is used to correct a procedural or clerical error made by the IRS.

82. __________ penalties may be applied if a taxpayer substantially understates their tax liability on their return.

83. The Taxpayer Bill of Rights includes the right to __________, ensuring taxpayers can find someone to assist if the IRS has not resolved their issues properly.

84. The IRS uses __________ letters to inform taxpayers that their tax return has been selected for audit.

85. __________ refers to the illegal act of not reporting all taxable income or inflating deductions to reduce tax liability.

86. A taxpayer must report changes in their __________ to the IRS if they are making payments under an installment agreement.

87. The __________ is responsible for investigating allegations of misconduct by tax professionals.

88. Circular 230 outlines the procedures for __________ a tax professional for violating its regulations.

89. The __________ rule is designed to ensure that advisors disclose certain tax shelter transactions to the IRS.

90. Taxpayers can request a(n) __________ from the IRS to determine the tax effects of their transactions or events before they occur.

91. The IRS may grant a(n) __________ to taxpayers affected by natural disasters, giving them additional time to file and pay taxes.

92. An __________ review is a process by which the IRS examines the tax returns of individuals who claim certain tax benefits to ensure they are entitled to them.

93. The IRS must notify the taxpayer in writing at least __________ days before levying their bank account.

94. __________ refers to a legal principle where a taxpayer cannot be tried twice for the same offense in tax matters.

95. The __________ is an annual report to Congress that highlights the most significant problems encountered by taxpayers.

96. Taxpayers can file a(n) __________ if they disagree with the IRS over the classification of a worker as an employee or independent contractor.

97. Practitioners are obligated to follow the __________ standards when providing written advice regarding federal tax matters.

98. The __________ is a process for taxpayers to dispute the classification of their debt as currently not collectible.

99. The IRS provides __________ transcripts, which include most of the line items from a filed tax return, to taxpayers upon request.

100. The __________ prohibits the IRS from disclosing a taxpayer's tax information without their consent, except as authorized by law.

101. The __________ is a measure that allows the IRS to collect an estimated tax deficiency directly from third parties who owe money to the taxpayer.

102. The __________ provides guidelines for tax practitioners regarding the use of estimates in preparing a tax return.

103. When a taxpayer submits new information in response to an IRS audit, the __________ must consider this information before making a final determination.

104. A tax practitioner who fails to comply with Circular 230 may face __________ as a disciplinary action.

105. The __________ requires the IRS to seal certain records if a taxpayer successfully completes an offer in compromise.

106. The __________ Act allows taxpayers to sue for damages if the IRS willfully or negligently fails to release a lien.

107. The __________ provides free tax help to people who generally make $60,000 or less, persons with disabilities, and limited English-speaking taxpayers.

108. The IRS uses __________ letters to notify taxpayers of potential discrepancies on their tax return.

109. Form __________ is required to submit an offer in compromise to the IRS.

110. The IRS may grant an __________ status to a taxpayer's account if they're unable to pay due to financial hardship.

111. A(n) __________ is a period of time in which the taxpayer can file a claim for a refund or the IRS can assess additional tax.

112. Tax-related identity theft victims should file Form __________ to report the issue to the IRS.

113. The IRS issues a __________ Notice of Deficiency to inform a taxpayer of its intention to assess additional tax.

114. A taxpayer may submit Form __________ to propose a settlement for their tax debt based on doubt as to collectibility.

115. To contest a lien or levy, taxpayers may request a Collection Due Process hearing by filing Form __________.

116. Form __________ is used by organizations applying for recognition of exemption under Section 501(c)(3).

EXTRA

OPEN-ENDED QUESTIONS

Extra Questions

1. What is the maximum income limit for a taxpayer to contribute to a Roth IRA for the tax year 2023 if their filing status is single?

2. A taxpayer contributes $4,000 to a traditional IRA. How much of this contribution is deductible if the taxpayer is covered by an employer-sponsored retirement plan?

3. What educational qualification is NOT a requirement for a taxpayer to claim the Lifetime Learning Credit?

4. What is the maximum amount of the Additional Child Tax Credit that can be refundable for the tax year 2023?

5. If a taxpayer inherits stocks and sells them after holding them for more than a year, what type of gain or loss is realized for tax purposes?

6. Which IRS form should a taxpayer use to report income earned as a freelancer or independent contractor?

7. What is the maximum amount a taxpayer can contribute to a Coverdell Education Savings Account (ESA) for the tax year 2023?

8. If a taxpayer pays $1,200 for qualified moving expenses due to a job relocation and the employer reimburses $800, what amount of moving expenses can the taxpayer deduct?

9. What is the age requirement for a taxpayer to withdraw funds from an IRA without incurring an early withdrawal penalty?

10. If a taxpayer contributes $3,500 to a Health Savings Account (HSA) for an individual, what is the maximum tax deduction available for this contribution?

11. What type of expenses can be deducted as a business expense for a self-employed individual?

____

____

____

12. What is the maximum income a taxpayer can earn to be eligible for the Premium Tax Credit for health insurance purchased through the Health Insurance Marketplace in 2023?

____

____

____

13. If a taxpayer receives a distribution from their 401(k) plan at age 40, how is this distribution taxed?

____

____

____

14. Which form should a taxpayer use to report income from interest earned on municipal bonds?

____

____

____

15. What is the maximum amount a taxpayer can contribute to a SIMPLE IRA for the tax year 2023 if they are under the age of 50?

____

____

____

16. If a taxpayer makes a non-deductible contribution to a traditional IRA, what portion of the withdrawal is taxable upon distribution?

17. What are the tax rates for long-term capital gains based on a taxpayer's income?

18. What is the maximum amount a taxpayer can contribute to a Health Savings Account (HSA) for a family for the tax year 2023?

19. If a taxpayer makes a non-deductible contribution to a traditional IRA, what portion of the withdrawal is taxable upon distribution?

20. What is the maximum amount of student loan interest a taxpayer can deduct for the tax year 2023 if their filing status is married filing jointly?

21. What is the maximum income limit for a taxpayer to qualify for the Savers Credit if filing as head of household in 2023?

22. A taxpayer sells a painting after owning it for 2 years, realizing a gain of $5,000. What type of gain is this for tax purposes?

23. What is the maximum contribution limit for a traditional IRA for the tax year 2023 if the taxpayer is over 50 years old?

24. What other conditions, besides having employment-related expenses and a qualifying dependent, must be satisfied to claim the Child and Dependent Care Credit?

25. How much of excess long-term capital losses can be used to offset ordinary income on a taxpayer's return??

26. Which IRS form should a taxpayer use to report income earned from dividends received during the tax year?

27. What is the maximum amount a taxpayer can contribute to a Health Flexible Spending Arrangement (FSA) for the tax year 2023?

28. If a taxpayer makes a charitable donation of $500 or more, what documentation is required to claim this deduction?

29. What is the maximum income limit for a taxpayer to qualify for the Savers Credit if filing as married couple filing jointly in 2023?

30. If a taxpayer contributes $2,000 to a Health Savings Account (HSA) for an individual, what is the maximum tax deduction available for this contribution?

31. List some of the expenses that are NOT deductible as medical expenses for tax purposes.

32. What is the maximum income a taxpayer can earn to be eligible for the American Opportunity Tax Credit for the tax year 2023?

33. Are distributions from a Roth IRA taxable?

34. Which form should a taxpayer use to report income from freelance work if they received payments of $600 or more during the tax year?

35. What is the maximum amount a taxpayer can contribute to a 401(k) plan for the tax year 2023 if they are under the age of 50?

36. If a taxpayer converts a traditional IRA to a Roth IRA, what tax event occurs?

37. What is the Earned Income Tax Credit (EITC)?

38. What is the maximum amount a taxpayer can contribute to a Dependent Care Flexible Spending Account (FSA) for the tax year 2023?

39. If a taxpayer contributes $3,000 to a traditional IRA, but their income exceeds the allowable limit for deductibility, what is the tax treatment of this contribution?

40. What are the limits for deducting home mortgage interest for loans taken out after December 15, 2017, compared to those for loans incurred before that date?

ANSWERS

PART 1 – INDIVIDUALS / MULTIPLE-CHOICE

Section 1: Preliminary Work and Taxpayer Data

1.Answer: c) Form 1099-NEC
2.Answer: b) Form 1099-INT
3.Answer: c) To calculate federal income tax withholding from employee paychecks
4.Answer: c) Individual Taxpayer Identification Number (ITIN)
5.Answer: d) To request a payment plan for tax liabilities they can't pay in full
6.Answer: c) To request a taxpayer's identification number for information reporting purposes
7.Answer: b) To change their address with the IRS
8.Answer: b) When they move to a new city
9.Answer: a) To request an extension of time to file taxes
10.Answer: c) Form 1099-DIV
11.Answer: b) $14,600
12.Answer: c) To report health insurance coverage information provided by an employer
13.Answer: d) A married couple filing jointly, one spouse 65 or older, with a gross income of $24,800
14.Answer: c) To authorize a representative to receive tax information
15.Answer: c) To report mortgage interest received or paid
16.Answer: c) To report independent contractor income
17.Answer: b) To file a complaint against a tax return preparer
18.Answer: c) To request a copy of a previously filed tax return
19.Answer: c) Widows with dependent children can file as Qualifying Widow(er) for two years following the year of their spouse's death; AND ALSO: d) Single filers include individuals who are divorced or legally separated according to state law at the end of the year.
20.Answer: c) To set up a payment plan for tax liabilities
21.Answer: b) To report dividend income from investments
22.Answer: b) To report interest paid on student loans
23.Answer: c) Social Security Number (SSN)
24.Answer: c) To report foreign financial assets
25.Answer: b) Undergraduates for the first four years of post-secondary education

26.Answer: b) Form 1099-G
27.Answer: b) To report tip income and allocated tips
28.Answer: a) To report income from investments
29.Answer: b) Schedule C
30.Answer: c) To correct errors on a previously filed tax return
31.Answer: c) To report income received through payment card or third-party network transactions
32.Answer: a) A taxpayer can claim a dependency exemption for a friend who has lived with them all year
33.Answer: a) April 15, 2024
34.Answer: b) To claim a tax credit for health coverage premiums
35.Answer: c) Unemployment compensation
36.Answer: b) They are filing as Married Filing Separately
37.Answer: c) To report IRA contributions made during the tax year
38.Answer: c) To report gifts exceeding the annual exclusion amount
39.Answer: c) The Age Test
40.Answer: d) To claim an exemption from the requirement to have health coverage

Section 2: Income and Assets

1.Answer: c) Ordinary income
2.Answer: c) To report income from self-employment or a sole proprietorship
3.Answer: c) U.S. Treasury bonds
4.Answer: c) To report gains or losses from the sale of business property
5.Answer: c) To report gains or losses from securities transactions
6.Answer: b) Schedule D
7.Answer: c) To report gains or losses from the sale of stocks, bonds, or real estate
8.Answer: b) To report gains from the sale of property where the seller receives payments over time
9.Answer: c) Form 1099-MISC
10.Answer: b) To report noncash donations exceeding $500
11.Answer: d) Schedule E (Form 1040)
12.Answer: b) To report gains or losses from the exchange of property
13.Answer: b) To report cancellation of debt exceeding $600
14.Answer: c) Schedule C (Form 1040)

15.Answer: b) To report the exercise of incentive stock options
16.Answer: c) Not taxable to the recipient and not deductible by the payer
17.Answer: d) Recovery period
18.Answer: c) To report specified foreign financial assets
19.Answer: c) Personal car
20.Answer: c) To report gains or losses from real estate transactions
21.Answer: b) 0%, 15%, or 20%, depending on the taxpayer's income
22.Answer: c) Alimony payments received under a divorce or separation agreement executed after 2018
23.Answer: d) $500,000
24.Answer: c) A portion may be taxable depending on other income
25.Answer: b) To calculate an alternative minimum tax amount
26.Answer: b) To report changes in corporate control or capital structure
27.Answer: a) Form 1099-B
28.Answer: b) To report undistributed long-term capital gains from a mutual fund
29.Answer: b) Interest income
30.Answer: b) To report losses from casualties or thefts
31.Answer: a) Form 1099-C
32.Answer: b) To report payments from qualified education programs
33.Answer: a) Form 1099-R
34.Answer: a) Original purchase price plus improvements
35.Answer: b) To report distributions from ABLE accounts
36.Answer: b) Form 1040
37.Answer: c) To report information about reportable policy sales
38.Answer: b) To report acquisition or abandonment of secured property
39.Answer: c) $3,000
40.Answer: c) An immediate expense deduction businesses can take for purchases of depreciable business equipment

Section 3: Deductions and Credits

1.Answer: c) Fully deductible as an itemized deduction
2.Answer: c) Form 2441
3.Answer: b) To claim a deduction for tuition and fees paid for higher education

4.Answer: b) To claim a credit for mortgage interest paid
5.Answer: d) Schedule EIC (Form 1040)
6.Answer: c) 60%
7.Answer: a) To claim a credit for retirement savings contributions
8.Answer: c) Form 8863
9.Answer: b) To claim a credit for health coverage premiums
10.Answer: b) To claim itemized deductions rather than the standard deduction
11.Answer: d) Schedule 8812 (Form 1040)
12.Answer: c) Work-related education expenses
13.Answer: b) To claim the Earned Income Credit
14.Answer: c) Tuition and enrollment fees
15.Answer: b) $15,950 (for 2023)
16.Answer: b) To allocate a tax refund into multiple accounts
17.Answer: a) Form 8880
18.Answer: a) $1,000
19.Answer: b) To claim the qualified business income deduction
20.Answer: b) $105,900
21.Answer: b) To claim an additional child tax credit
22.Answer: b) To amend a previously filed tax return
23.Answer: b) Costs of Solar Electric Property and Solar Water Heaters
24.Answer: b) To report student loan interest paid
25.Answer: b) To claim a credit for a qualified plug-in electric drive motor vehicle
26.Answer: c) It can be used for undergraduate, graduate, and professional degree courses
27.Answer: c) Both A and B
28.Answer: b) To claim education-related tax credits
29.Answer: b) $29,200
30.Answer: a) 7.5%
31.Answer: b) $7,000
32.Answer: c) Entertainment expenses related to business
33.Answer: b) To exclude interest from certain savings bonds
34.Answer: b) To claim deductions for noncash charitable contributions
35.Answer: b) Child Tax Credit
36.Answer: b) To claim residential energy efficiency tax credits
37.Answer: b) To report withholding tax on dispositions of U.S. real property interests

38.Answer: c) Have earned income and adjusted gross income within certain limits
39.Answer: b) To claim a credit for alternative motor vehicle purchases
40.Answer: b) To track nondeductible IRA contributions

Section 4: Taxation and Advice

1.Answer: b) To report withholding of federal income tax on non-payroll payments
2.Answer: c) To report miscellaneous income not included on other information returns
3.Answer: b) 20%
4.Answer: b) To report nonemployee compensation exceeding $600
5.Answer: b) 3.8%
6.Answer: c) Life insurance proceeds
7.Answer: b) To report cash payments exceeding $10,000 received in a trade or business
8.Answer: b) $13.61 million
9.Answer: b) Form 1099-INT
10.Answer: c) Medical expenses above 10% of AGI
11.Answer: b) To substitute for a missing or incorrect Form W-2 or 1099-R
12.Answer: a) To report gambling winnings
13.Answer: b) To report distributions from various retirement or pension plans
14.Answer: b) To claim a credit for taxes paid to foreign countries
15.Answer: b) Double taxation on foreign income
16.Answer: b) To request a transcript of a previously filed tax return
17.Answer: b) To summarize and transmit various information returns to the IRS
18.Answer: c) The penalty for not having health insurance was eliminated in 2019 for federal taxes
19.Answer: b) To estimate and pay quarterly taxes for individuals with income not subject to withholding
20.Answer: b) To claim exemptions from health coverage requirements
21.Answer: c) 24
22.Answer: a) The excess is refunded up to $1,600 per qualifying child as the additional child tax credit
23.Answer: a) 24%
24.Answer: a) $250,000

25.Answer: b) To report certain government payments like unemployment compensation or state tax refunds
26.Answer: b) To report income from a corporation
27.Answer: d) $120,000
28.Answer: b) To report proceeds from real estate transactions exceeding $600
29.Answer: b) To report excise taxes on specific goods, services, and activities
30.Answer: c) Qualified dividends
31.Answer: b) It allows for the deduction of personal exemptions
32.Answer: b) To report quarterly employment taxes
33.Answer: a) January 15, 2025
34.Answer: b) To report mortgage interest paid by an individual
35.Answer: d) $15,950
36.Answer: c) 5%
37.Answer: b) To specify the amount of federal income tax to be withheld from an employee's paycheck
38.Answer: b) To request an extension for certain business income tax returns
39.Answer: c) $200,000 for single filers
40.Answer: a) A 20-year-old full-time college student with unearned income of $2,500
41.Answer: b) To notify the IRS of a change of address
42.Answer: c) Net earnings from self-employment
43.Answer: a) 0.9%
44.Answer: b) To report contributions made to an IRA
45.Answer: d) Qualifying Widow(er)

Section 5: Advising the Individual Taxpayer

1.Answer: b) To claim a credit for child and dependent care expenses
2.Answer: b) To reconcile and claim the premium tax credit
3.Answer: c) Form 1099-SA
4.Answer: b) To report distributions from Archer MSAs and long-term care insurance contracts
5.Answer: b) Mortgage interest and property taxes
6.Answer: d) The total amount of itemizable deductions exceeds the standard deduction

7.Answer: a) Aggregating medical procedures into a single tax year to exceed the AGI threshold for deduction
8.Answer: b) American Opportunity Tax Credit
9.Answer: b) Making annual gifts up to the federal gift tax exclusion limit
10.Answer: b) To report interest income earned during the tax year
11.Answer: b) To claim a deduction for casualty and theft losses
12.Answer: b) A traditional IRA
13.Answer: b) The distribution may be subject to a 10% early withdrawal penalty
14.Answer: b) To claim a credit for qualified retirement savings contributions
15.Answer: b) Form 1099-S
16.Answer: b) To report qualified disaster-related retirement plan distributions
17.Answer: a) Be a U.S. citizen or resident
18.Answer: b) To claim residential energy-efficient property credits
19.Answer: b) To report net investment income subject to the Net Investment Income Tax
20.Answer: a) Donating appreciated stock held for more than one year to avoid capital gains tax
21.Answer: b) To report distributions from education savings accounts
22.Answer: b) Contribute to a SEP IRA
23.Answer: c) The converted amount is taxable in the year of the conversion
24.Answer: b) To claim deductions for business use of a home
25.Answer: b) To report contributions and distributions from an HSA
26.Answer: b) The home was the taxpayer's primary residence for at least 2 of the last 5 years
27.Answer: b) To report gains or losses from the sale of capital assets
28.Answer: c) There are higher contribution limits
29.Answer: a) Investing in municipal bonds
30.Answer: c) Determining which parent can claim a child as a dependent
31.Answer: b) To claim expenses related to adopting a child
32.Answer: c) Expenses and depreciation can offset rental income
33.Answer: c) Contributions to a qualified nonprofit organization
34.Answer: b) Holding investments long-term to qualify for capital gains treatment
35.Answer: d) A and B

36.Answer: a) Gifting assets up to the annual exclusion amount each year to family members
37.Answer: b) To calculate alternative minimum tax liability
38.Answer: c) Are tax-deductible and withdrawals for qualified medical expenses are tax-free
39.Answer: b) Increasing their 401(k) contributions
40.Answer: c) A 429 plan
41.Answer: b) Preferential capital gains rates
42.Answer: b) To calculate and report passive activity loss limitations
43.Answer: a) Traditional IRA
44.Answer: d) All of the above
45.Answer: a) Reduce the number of allowances claimed on their W-4

Section 6: Specialized Returns for Individuals

1.Answer: b) To claim the foreign-earned income exclusion
2.Answer: a) 5695
3.Answer: c) Taxpayers age 65 or older
4.Answer: b) To report installment sale income from selling property
5.Answer: c) Schedule F (Form 1040)
6.Answer: b) Form 1040-X
7.Answer: b) To claim credits for investment in certain qualified properties
8.Answer: a) Power of attorney
9.Answer: a) Moving expenses for members of the Armed Forces
10.Answer: b) To report a child's interest and dividend income on the parent's return
11.Answer: a) 8839
12.Answer: b) To calculate and report at-risk limitations for certain activities
13.Answer: b) Foreign-earned income exclusion
14.Answer: b) Request an automatic extension to file
15.Answer: a) Form 1040-NR
16.Answer: b) To disclose a position taken on a tax treaty
17.Answer: c) Schedule D (Form 1040)
18.Answer: .b) FinCEN Form 114 (FBAR)
19.Answer: a) Claim a child's unearned income on their own tax return
20.Answer: a) First-Time Homebuyer Credit

21.Answer: b) To report noncash charitable contributions
22.Answer: b) To calculate and report tax for children with significant investment income
23.Answer: a) A child has unearned income above a certain threshold
24.Answer: b) To elect to be treated as an S corporation for tax purposes
25.Answer: b) To report information about a foreign partnership interest
26.Answer: d) Both A and B
27.Answer: b) To report information about certain foreign corporations
28.Answer: a) Release/revocation of the release of claim to exemption for a child by the custodial parent.
29.Answer: a) Form 1040 Schedule F
30.Answer: b) Schedule E
31.Answer: b) To disclose information about certain Canadian retirement plans
32.Answer: b) Form 1041
33.Answer: a) Form 2555
34.Answer: a) 1116
35.Answer: d) They can no longer deduct these expenses due to changes in tax law
36.Answer: b) To claim an exemption from withholding on compensation for nonresident aliens
37.Answer: a) Gift taxes
38.Answer: a) Schedule SE
39.Answer: b) To report cash payments received over $10,000 in a trade or business
40.Answer: b) To report information about foreign disregarded entities
41.Answer: a) Form 6251
42.Answer: b) Additional taxes on qualified plans
43.Answer: b) Exclusively and regularly as your principal place of business
44.Answer: a) Form 4797
45.Answer: b) To calculate and report net investment income tax

PART 1: INDIVIDUALS / FILL IN THE BLANK

1. April 15, 2024
2. $13,850
3. $6,500
4. $6,604
5. $17,000
6. $1,850
7. 5%
8. $153,000
9. $2,500
10. 60%
11. 65,5 cents per mile
12. $2,000
13. 18
14. $695 or 2.5% of household income, whichever is higher
15. $4,700
16. $116,000
17. 15.3%
18. $15,950
19. 100%, 110%
20. $182,100
21. Form 8889
22. $0 (The individual mandate penalty was reduced to $0 starting in 2019, but some states may have their own penalties.)
23. $167,800
24. $6,000
25. 7.5%
26. $7,500
27. 20%
28. $330,000
29. 2%
30. 70½ (changed to 72 for those turning 70½ after December 31, 2019, but still relevant for some)
31. $250,000, $500,000

32. $7,750
33. $36,000
34. $3,000
35. 3.8%
36. $12,920,000
37. $2,000
38. $16,500
39. $36,500
40. $0
41. 15%
42. June 17, 2024
43. 73
44. 100%
45. 50%
46. $15,500
47. 50%
48. $7,500
49. $2,000
50. 100%, 400%
51. 400% of the federal poverty line (specific dollar amount varies by family size and state)
52. 25%, $66,000
53. 22 cents
54. $17,000
55. 10%
56. $2,000,000
57. $5,250
58. $13,850
59. $75,000
60. $1,600
61. $160,000
62. $10,000
63. $300 ($600 for married filing jointly)
64. 3
65. 13
66. $22,500

67. $10,000
68. 100%
69. disaster
70. 8
71. $450
72. $228,000
73. 18
74. $6,500
75. $182,100
76. $56,838
77. $120,000 + applicable housing exclusion
78. $27,700
79. $1,000
80. $7,000. If you are 50 and older, you can contribute an additional $1,000 for a total of $8,000
81. $600
82. $175,000
83. 50
84. $1,000
85. $1,250
86. 35%
87. $22,500
88. 30
89. $1,500
90. No limit
91. 14
92. $376.92
93. $150,000
94. $3,050
95. 35%
96. $80,000, $160,000
97. $7,430
98. $11,000
99. $1,850, $1,500
100. $81,300

101. $10,000

102. $25

103. 0.5%

104. 17

105. $1,000

106. already taxed

107. Not applicable (Miscellaneous itemized deductions subject to the 2% floor were suspended under the Tax Cuts and Jobs Act for tax years 2018 through 2025.)

108. 10

109. W-4

110. 8822

111. Standard

112. Inflation

113. C

114. Unemployment

115. Married

116. Age

117. 1040-X

118. Head

119. 8962

120. Unearned

121. Four

122. 4868

123. $185,000

PART 2 – BUSINESSES / MULTIPLE-CHOICE

Section 1: Businesses

1.c) Limited Liability Company (LLC)
2.c) Section 1361
3.b) 100
4.b) Form 1065
5.a) Calendar year
6.b) 21%
7.b) Limited liability protection for all partners
8.c) Form 1120
9.d) Partnership
10.b) 8832
11.a) Unlimited
12.c) C Corporation
13.b) Partially taxable
14.d) Sole Proprietorship
15.b) C Corporations
16.b) Manufacture products or purchase them for resale
17.c) It is taxed as a partnership
18.d) Limited partner
19.d) Carry the loss back or forward, depending on the tax laws in effect
20.b) Pass-through taxation
21.b) Limited liability for shareholders
22.b) 21%
23.b) Form SS-4
24.c) Both Social Security and Medicare taxes
25.c) To establish the corporation with the state
26.b) FICA and FUTA
27.b) It is taxed only at the individual partner level
28.b) S Corporations, partnerships, sole proprietorships, and LLCs.
29.c) Excise tax
30.d) Corporation

31.b) 2553
32.b) One general partner and one limited partner
33.c) 310
34.c) Ordinary and necessary
35.c) Increase spending on qualifying research activities.
36.b) Income and losses are passed through to shareholders
37.b) Offshore corporation
38.b) Officers
39.b) Pass-through taxation like an S Corporation
40.b) Calculating and reporting depreciation and amortization.
41.b) 51%
42.b) As a partnership
43.b) Accrual
44.c) Income is taxed only at the individual level
45.d) Form 1120S
46.b) Disregarded entities
47.c) In proportion to their ownership percentage
48.c) 21%
49.b) A trust fund recovery penalty.
50.a) Limited Liability Company (LLC)
51.a) $100 per month per partner
52.c) An Employer Identification Number (EIN)
53.c) 100%
54.c) Targeted groups
55.b) The cost of the property plus any improvements minus depreciation.
56.b) Can be a fiscal year that is different from the calendar year
57.c) C Corporation
58.b) Considered a tax-free return of capital to the extent of the partner's basis in the partnership.
59.b) Its income and losses are passed through to shareholders
60.d) Prevent businesses from retaining excess earnings to avoid paying dividends to shareholders

Section 2: Business Financial Information

1.c) Income statement
2.b) Earnings Before Interest, Taxes, Depreciation and Amortization

3.d) Cash, accounts receivable, and marketable securities
4.c) Quick Ratio
5.d) Equity Multiplier
6.a) Inventory Turnover Ratio
7.c) Higher financial leverage
8.a) Balance sheet
9.b) C Corporation
10.a) Total Assets
11.a) Accounts Receivable Turnover Ratio
12.b) Higher profitability relative to its asset base
13.a) Earnings Before Taxes
14.b) Shareholders' Equity
15.b) Interest Coverage Ratio
16.a) Form 4797
17.c) Fully deductible as a business expense
18.a) Net Income / Average Total Assets
19.c) Higher financial risk
20.a) 50%
21.a) Return on Assets (ROA)
22.d) It applies to income from sole proprietorships, S corporations, partnerships, and LLCs.
23.b) Treated as a distribution from earnings and profits
24.a) Efficient inventory management
25.a) March 15
26.b) Net Income / Shareholders' Equity
27.a) Acid-Test Ratio
28.b) Higher expected earnings growth
29.a) Asset Turnover and Profit Margin
30.b) Certain new and used property placed in service after September 27, 2017
31.c) Section 179
32.c) Financial leverage
33.b) S Corporations
34.a) Current assets by current liabilities
35.a) A company's ability to generate profit from its shareholders' investment
36.a) Cost of goods sold by average inventory

37.c) Gross profit by net sales
38.c) Charitable contributions
39.a) Total liabilities by total assets
40.b) March 15
41.a) The liquidity of a company
42.a) Form W-2
43.c) Operating cash flow by total assets
44.b) Form 8829
45.a) How efficiently a company uses its assets
46.c) Efficiency in using assets
47.d) Indefinitely
48.a) The ratio of gross profit to total revenue
49.c) To measure the company's financial leverage
50.b) The efficiency in collecting cash from customers
51.a) Debt ratio
52.b) To assess the company's liquidity position
53.a) How effectively a company manages its inventory
54.b) Cash and near-cash assets to cover current liabilities
55.B. $20,200
56.a) The efficiency of using assets to generate sales
57.c) Federal income tax withholdings, Social Security, and Medicare taxes
58.b) The market price of a stock relative to its earnings per share
59.b) Profit Margin
60.c) Cash Conversion Cycle

Section 3: Specialized Returns and Taxpayers

1.d) Both A and B
2.d) December
3.b) Line 8b
4.a) Form 2290
5.b) Claim foreign tax credit
6.d) As specified in the operating agreement
7.a) Form 4720
8.b) Reportable transaction understatement.
9.c) A partnership.

10.a) Additional taxes on IRAs and other tax-favored accounts
11.a) Form 2553
12.c) Reporting income from S corporations
13.b) Form 1041
14.c) Individuals
15.a) Form 8889
16.a) a) Form 1128
17.a) Form 4136
18.a) Schedule K-1 (Form 1065)
19.a) Form 3115
20.c) Form 5471
21.a) September 15
22.a) The investment credit
23.a) The state's taxation department
24.a) 8886
25.c) Form 990-T
26.a) Cash payments over $10,000 received in a trade or business.
27.d) Form 8804
28.b) Employee benefit plan reporting
29.d) Form 8938
30.c) $6,000
31.a) Quarterly Federal Excise Taxes
32.b) 13 years old
33.a) Schedule F
34.a) Form 990
35.a) Form W-2G
36.b) $60,000
37.a) Form 1023
38.b) Schedule J
39.a) Form 1041
40.b) $2,000
41.b) Reporting income from a trust or estate
42.a) Making them non-deductible by the payer and non-taxable to the recipient
43.d) Qualifying widow(er) with dependent child
44.a) Form 8839

45.a) Form 1040 Schedule R
46.c) Both A and B
47.d) The unearned income of children under age 19 / full-time students under age 24
48.b) Unrelated business taxable income
49.a) Form 2106
50.a) December 15
51.c) Form 1066
52.d) $3,850
53.c) Form 1120-REIT
54.b) Form 1120-FSC
55.c) Exempt from federal income tax but subject to self-employment tax
56.a) Form 1120-POL
57.b) May 15
58.d) Both A and B
59.a) Form 6765
60.b) Taxpayers whose gifts to any one individual exceed the annual exclusion amount

PART 2: BUSINESSES / FILL IN THE BLANK

1. $1,160,000
2. 10
3. April 15, 2024
4. 21 percent
5. $66,000 or 25 percent
6. $310
7. 20 percent
8. 25
9. $7,500
10. 50 percent
11. Straight-line
12. 20 percent
13. $25 million
14. 10 percent
15. 25 percent
16. 50 percent
17. 80 percent
18. 50 percent, $5,000
19. $2.90 million
20. 100
21. January 31, 2024
22. 7 years
23. 50 percent
24. 37.5 percent
25. 1.39 percent
26. 250
27. $250,000
28. $20,200
29. 50-65 percent
30. 30 percent
31. 100 percent
32. 15.3 percent
33. 60 percent

34. 73
35. $5,000
36. $30 million
37. $200,000
38. 27.5 years
39. July 31, 2024
40. 31 days
41. 20
42. 80 percent
43. $29 million
44. 5 (beginning in 2018, new farm equipment under the Tax Cuts and Jobs Act)
45. $275,000 or 100
46. $200,000
47. $26 million
48. $265,000 or 100
49. March 15
50. $309
51. $64
52. 0 (Note: the "Cadillac tax" had been repealed and is not applicable.)
53. 25
54. 9
55. representative
56. 50, $10,250
57. $74
58. $12,200
59. $2,500
60. 39
61. $9,600
62. 100
63. $400
64. 100, not deductible
65. $5 million
66. 5 percent, 25 percent
67. $1.80
68. $29 million

69. 50 percent
70. No specific limit, but generally tailored for smaller businesses
71. 15 or over 180 months
72. $19,500
73. 25
74. third
75. $310
76. February 14
77. 4626, 2022
78. $3,850
79. January 15, 2024
80. $2,500
81. $66,000
82. 15
83. $19,000
84. $500,000
85. 25
86. 0 (since the carryback of NOLs was largely eliminated except for farming losses and certain insurance companies)
87. $50,000
88. 12, $25,000
89. 60 percent
90. 100 percent
91. 100
92. The inflation adjustment factor is not a percentage but a numerical value used to adjust certain tax parameters; specific values apply annually.
93. 5
94. $160,200
95. 80 percent
96. $22,500
97. 1120S
98. Limited Liability Company (LLC)
99. 1099-NEC
100. 940
101. Withholding

102. Modified Accelerated Cost Recovery System (MACRS)
103. 6765
104. Cash
105. Payroll
106. SS-4
107. 1128
108. 941
109. 50 percent
110. 40 percent
111. 10 percent
112. $69,000
113. $23,000
114. $11,700

PART 3 – REPRESENTATION / MULTIPLE-CHOICE

Section 1: Practices and Procedures

1.c) 3 years
2.b) 3 years
3.d) Taxpayer representation before a Revenue Officer
4.b) Form 2848
5.a) Filing tax returns electronically
6.d) Taxpayer
7.a) 12153
8.d) None of the above
9.b) Form 4868
10.a) Complete Form 656
11.b) Identify a tax professional authorized to access taxpayer information
12.c) To assist taxpayers facing hardships
13.d) All of the above
14.a) 4 weeks
15.b) Prior work experience with the IRS
16.c) Governs practice before the IRS
17.c) To authorize disclosure of information to third parties
18.c) An abatement of tax-related penalties
19.d) All of the above
20.a) American Institute of Certified Public Accountants
21.a) Obtain a PTIN
22.b) Providing expanded access to installment agreements and Offers in Compromise
23.b) Employer Identification Number
24.a) Form 9465
25.c) 10
26.b) To represent a taxpayer before the IRS
27.a) AICPA
28.c) Responsible individuals who willfully fail to collect or pay employment taxes

29.a) $50
30.c) Before engaging in representation
31.a) Access to tax return information
32.c) Professionals who prepare tax returns for compensation
33.a) 8857
34.a) CP2000
35.c) Both A and B
36.c) Ethical and practice standards for tax professionals
37.b) IRS
38.b) Digital tax return fling services
39.b) Electronically sign a tax return
40.b) File tax returns on behalf of clients
41.d) Within 21 days
42.c) Oversee the ethical conduct of tax professionals
43.a) 5% of the tax due per month
44.c) Tax professionals authorized to represent taxpayers before the IRS
45.b) Notify the IRS of change of address

Section 2: Representation before the IRS

1.b) Settle their tax debt for less than the full amount owed
2.d) To authorize someone to represent them before the IRS
3.b) 10 years from the assessment date
4.b) Power of Attorney
5.d) All of the above
6.b) An offer in compromise
7.c) Enrolled Agent
8.b) Help taxpayers with overdue taxes by offering flexible payment options
9.a) Every year
10.c) Request a conference with the auditor's manager
11.c) Completing a degree in accounting
12.b) Continuing education requirements
13.a) Form 8822
14.d) All of the above
15.a) The Taxpayer Bill of Rights

16.c) Seek help resolving tax problems that haven't been resolved through normal channels
17.a) 2 years
18.c) Tax professionals authorized to practice before the IRS
19.c) If the written communication is furnished to a client regarding tax advice
20.c) $5,000
21.b) Provide all relevant documents to facilitate the audit
22.b) Achieve the best outcome for the taxpayer
23.c) Correct the errors and discuss options with the taxpayer
24.b) A dedicated phone service for tax professionals to obtain assistance with client issues
25.a) Only with the taxpayer's written consent
26.a) Charge a contingent fee for services related to an IRS audit
27.b) Notify all clients immediately and cease representation
28.b) An independent organization within the IRS
29.b) To ensure accurate and complete tax flings
30.c) Work impartially to resolve conflicts
31.b) Failing to provide a copy of a tax return to a client
32.c) Communicate clearly and manage client expectations realistically
33.c) Individuals authorized to practice before the IRS
34.c) When the tax issue is resolved
35.b) When the taxpayer's spouse is involved in the issue
36.d) There is no monetary penalty specified
37.c) Correct the error and inform the client about the necessary steps
38.d) When the taxpayer doesn't pay the representation fees
39.c) To establish guidelines for practitioners' conduct in representing taxpayers
40.c) To ensure compliance with tax laws while advocating for the taxpayer's rights
41.b) When the taxpayer is represented by an attorney
42.c) Offers guidance for tax professionals representing taxpayers before the IRS
43.c) Exercising thoroughness and accuracy in preparing and advising on tax matters
44.d) When the representation becomes unreasonably difficult or impracticable
45.b) Tax practitioners can't represent a taxpayer if they previously represented the IRS on the same matter

Section 3: Specific Types of Representation

1.a) Offer in Compromise
2.b) To grant power of attorney for IRS representation
3.b) Appeal to the Office of Appeals
4.a) To claim a refund or abatement of taxes, penalties, and interest
5.a) The opportunity to appeal the denial of an Offer in Compromise
6.a) Form 656
7.d) To request assistance during a significant financial hardship
8.a) Currently Not Collectible
9.a) Request for a taxpayer advocate
10.b) If they believe their spouse or former spouse should be solely responsible for a tax bill
11.a) Form 12153
12.d) To apply for a payment plan
13.a) To request an Installment Agreement
14.c) Offer in Compromise
15.c) To request a Collection Due Process hearing
16.b) Form 8857
17.b) Matters before the IRS, but not in Tax Court
18.a) Separate a taxpayer's liability from that of their spouse or ex-spouse
19.c) To provide more time to pay tax debts
20.a) Form 843
21.a) To claim a refund of interest and penalties
22.c) 90 days to petition the Tax Court without paying the disputed amount
23.b) Form 941-X
24.c) Providing financial information for a Collection Alternative
25.a) Form 433-A (OIC)
26.b) May be discharged, depending on the type of tax and timing of the bankruptcy
27.c) The practices of tax professionals authorized to represent taxpayers
28.c) To temporarily suspend IRS collection actions
29.a) Collection Due Process (CDP)
30.b) Pre-filing Agreement Program
31.c) Low-Income Taxpayer Clinics (LITCs)
32.b) Preparing a taxpayer's return

33.d) To request a Collection Due Process hearing
34.a) Pass a special tax court exam
35.c) Large Business and International Division
36.c) To settle tax debts for less than the full amount
37.b) Enrolled agents who pass the Tax Court's examination
38.b) Complete a specific number of continuing education hours annually
39.b) They were unaware of their spouse's understatement of tax
40.b) Business owners responsible for unpaid employment taxes
41.b) Form 12153
42.b) Form 843
43.d) To request a Collection Due Process hearing
44.b) To claim a refund of taxes, interest, or penalties
45.c) To request Taxpayer Advocate Service assistance

Section 4: Completion of the Filing Process

1.c) Provide financial information to the IRS to set up a payment plan or compromise
2.c) Propose a settlement for less than the full amount of taxes owed
3.d) October 15
4.a) Delaying refunds for taxpayers claiming the Earned Income Tax Credit (EITC) or Additional Child Tax Credit (ACTC) until February 15
5.c) Form 12203, Request for Appeals Review
6.b) To request withdrawal of a filed Notice of Federal Tax Lien
7.a) Notify the IRS of the creation or termination of a fiduciary relationship
8.c) Online Account
9.b) Currently Not Collectible status
10.b) February 15
11.c) Schedule B (Form 1040)
12.c) Form 1040-ES
13.d) Form 1098
14.b) Making estimated tax payments for individuals
15.b) 1127
16.c) Reporting miscellaneous income

17.b) Independent contractors for non-employee compensation
18.b) Paying federal taxes online or by phone
19.d) Assessment statute expiration date
20.a) Form 4506
21.c) PayPal
22.c) Calculating Premium Tax Credit
23.d) $0 starting from the tax year 2019
24.a) 4868
25.c) An acknowledgment letter
26.b) FinCEN Form 114, FBAR
27.a) 18 hours of continuing education including a six-hour federal tax law update course
28.b) File an amended return immediately to correct the mistake
29.c) Publication 594
30.a) Single
31.b) Application for Automatic Extension of Time to File U.S. Individual Income Tax Return
32.c) To inform the IRS of a taxpayer's new address
33.b) Requires special software or a tax professional
34.b) Form 8949
35.b) 5% of the tax due per month, up to 25%
36.c) Office of Appeals
37.b) 10% of the underpayment amount
38.a) File a police report and notify the IRS immediately
39.a) An installment agreement for paying taxes owed
40.a) 21 days of e-filing
41.b) An option that can speed up refund processing
42.b) Proves that the levy is causing an economic hardship
43.a) The "Where's My Refund?" tool on the IRS website
44.b) A paper check
45.b) There is a proposed change based on a mismatch between income reported by the taxpayer and information returns

PART 3: REPRESENTATION / FILL IN THE BLANK

1. identical
2. Competence
3. endorsing fraudulent documents
4. October
5. $1,000
6. 3
7. Right to Pay No More than the Correct Amount of Tax
8. Right to Challenge the IRS's Position and Be Heard
9. tax professionals
10. Enrolled Agents
11. doubt as to liability, doubt as to collectibility
12. pay back taxes, avoid tax liens
13. retain
14. Internal Revenue Code
15. audit
16. deductions
17. Appeals Office
18. nature and amount
19. integrity
20. District Court
21. Taxpayer Advocate Service
22. $225
23. Taxpayer Advocate Service
24. notice of deficiency
25. John Doe
26. 16,2
27. 72
28. check
29. comply
30. confidential communications
31. installment agreement
32. Treasury Inspector General for Tax Administration (TIGTA)
33. levy action

34. Economic substance
36. Federal Tort Claims Act
37. civil
38. Collection Statute Expiration Date (CSED)
39. voluntary
40. protest
41. tax system
42. administrative
43. written consent
44. practice before the IRS
45. IRS Restructuring and Reform Act of 1998
46. Office of Appeals
47. disbarred or suspended
48. taxpayer-practitioner
49. due diligence
50. 6
51. Tax Court
52. Saver's or Retirement Savings Contributions
53. transparency
54. reasonable
55. Tax preparer fraud
56. Identity Protection PIN (IP PIN)
57. frivolous arguments
58. Right to Be Informed
59. disclose
60. Collection Information Statement
61. Notice of Deficiency
62. Where's My Amended Return
63. Offset
64. disbarred practitioners list
65. Tax Account Transcript
66. Streamlined Filing Compliance Procedures
67. Power of Attorney (Form 2848)
68. Foreign Account Tax Compliance Act (FATCA)
69. Taxpayer Bill of Rights

70. Taxpayer Bill of Rights
71. third-party contact notice
72. disposition
73. 8821
74. original
75. lock-in letter
76. failure-to-file
77. 30
78. conference
79. reasonable
80. 10
81. adjustment
82. Accuracy-related
83. Finality
84. examination
85. Tax evasion
86. financial situation
87. Office of Professional Responsibility (OPR)
88. sanctioning
89. reportable transaction
90. private letter ruling
91. disaster relief extension
92. compliance
93. 30
94. Double jeopardy
95. Annual Report to Congress
96. SS-8
97. applicable law
98. Collection Appeal Program (CAP)
99. tax return
100. Confidentiality of Information
101. levy action
102. due diligence requirements
103. auditor
104. censure, suspension, or disbarment

105. Fresh Start initiative
106. Taxpayer Bill of Rights Act
107. Volunteer Income Tax Assistance (VITA) program
108. CP2000
109. 656-L
110. Currently Not Collectible (CNC)
111. statute of limitations
112. 14039
113. 90-day
114. Form 656
115. Form 12153
116. Form 1023

EXTRA / OPEN-ENDED

1. The maximum income limit for a taxpayer to contribute to a Roth IRA for the tax year 2023 if their filing status is single is subject to phase-out rules, beginning at $138,000 and ending at $153,000.

2. If the taxpayer is covered by an employer-sponsored retirement plan, the deductible contribution depends on the Modified Adjusted Gross Income (MAGI). It's subject to phase-out, beginning at $77,000 and ending at $87,000 for the tax year 2023.

3. Being enrolled in a degree program is NOT a requirement for a taxpayer to claim the Lifetime Learning Credit.

4. The maximum amount of the Additional Child Tax Credit that can be refundable for the tax year 2023 is $1,600 per qualifying child.

5. If a taxpayer inherits stocks and sells them after holding them for more than a year, it generates a long-term capital gain or loss for tax purposes.

6. A taxpayer should use Schedule C of Form 1040 to report income earned as a freelancer or independent contractor.

7. The maximum amount a taxpayer can contribute to a Coverdell Education Savings Account (ESA) for the tax year 2023 is $2,000.

8. The taxpayer can deduct $400 of moving expenses ($1,200 paid - $800 reimbursed).

9. The age requirement for a taxpayer to withdraw funds from an IRA without incurring an early withdrawal penalty is 59½ years old.

10. If a taxpayer contributes $3,500 to a Health Savings Account (HSA) for an individual, the maximum tax deduction available for this contribution is $3,500.

11. Home Office, Office Supplies and Equipment, Travel and Meals, Vehicle Use, Salaries and Benefits, Rent, Utilities, Insurance, Professional Services, Marketing and Advertising, Education and Training, Interest, Taxes and Licenses.

12. It's based on household income and is generally available to individuals and families with household incomes between 100% and 400% of the federal poverty level (FPL). 400% of the FPL in 203 is $54,360

13. If a taxpayer receives a distribution from their 401(k) plan at age 40, it is subject to ordinary income tax and a 10% early withdrawal penalty unless an exception applies.

14. Form 1099-INT should be used to report income from interest earned on municipal bonds.

15. The maximum amount a taxpayer can contribute to a SIMPLE IRA for the tax year 2023 if they are under the age of 50 is $15,500.

16. Upon distribution, the portion of the withdrawal from a traditional IRA that represents non-deductible contributions is not taxable; only the earnings and deductible contributions are taxable.

17. The Capital Gains Tax Rate for long-term investments can range from 0% to 20%, depending on the taxpayer's income.

18. The maximum amount a taxpayer can contribute to a Health Savings Account (HSA) for a family for the tax year 2023 is $7,750.

19. The portion of the withdrawal representing non-deductible contributions to a traditional IRA is not taxable; earnings and deductible contributions are taxable upon distribution.

20. The maximum amount of student loan interest a taxpayer can deduct for the tax year 2023 if their filing status is married filing jointly is $2,500.

21. The maximum income limit for a taxpayer to qualify for the Savers Credit if filing as head of household in 2023 is $54,750.

22. A gain of $5,000 from selling a painting after owning it for 2 years is considered a short-term capital gain for tax purposes.

23. The maximum contribution limit for a traditional IRA for the tax year 2023 if the taxpayer is over 50 years old is $7,500.

24. The additional condition that must be met to claim the Child and Dependent Care Credit is that the expenses must be incurred to enable the taxpayer (and spouse, if filing jointly) to work or actively look for work.

25. Excess long-term capital losses can be used to offset ordinary income up to a maximum of $3,000 per year ($1,500 if married filing separately).

26. Form 1099-DIV is used to report income earned from dividends received during the tax year.

27. The maximum amount a taxpayer can contribute to a Health Flexible Spending Arrangement (FSA) for the tax year 2023 is $3,050.

28. A written acknowledgment from the charity is required for charitable donations of $250 or more to claim this deduction.

29. In 2023, for a married couple filing jointly to qualify for the Saver's Credit, the maximum income limit is $73,000.

30. If a taxpayer contributes $2,000 to a Health Savings Account (HSA) for an individual, the maximum tax deduction available for this contribution is $2,000.

31. Non-deductible health-related expenses typically include nonprescription drugs (except insulin), toothpaste, health club memberships, vitamins, diet foods, and nonprescription nicotine products.

32. Full credit requires a MAGI of $80,000 or less ($160,000 if married filing jointly), with reduced credit for MAGIs between $80,000-$90,000 ($160,000-$180,000 for joint filers).

33. A qualified distribution from a Roth IRA is tax-free, as it was funded with after-tax dollars.

34. Form 1099-MISC is used to report income from freelance work if payments of $600 or more were received during the tax year.

35. The maximum amount a taxpayer can contribute to a 401(k) plan for the tax year 2023 if they are under the age of 50 is $22,500.

36. Converting a traditional IRA to a Roth IRA counts the converted amount as taxable income, possibly raising that year's tax liability..

37. The Earned Income Tax Credit (EITC) is a refundable credit designed to assist low to moderate-income earners.

38. The maximum amount a taxpayer can contribute to a Dependent Care Flexible Spending Account (FSA) for the tax year 2023 is $5,000.

39. Contributions exceeding income limits for a traditional IRA become non-deductible but stay in the account.

40. Deduct mortgage interest on up to $750,000 of debt ($375,000 if filing separately), or up to $1 million ($500,000 if filing separately) for debt from before December 16, 2017.

APPENDIX

2023 Tax Brackets

2023 Tax Brackets

Annually, the Internal Revenue Service (IRS) updates over 60 tax provisions to account for inflation, mitigating "bracket creep." This phenomenon occurs when inflation causes individuals to move into higher tax brackets or diminishes the value of their credits and deductions, not due to actual increases in income. Before 2018, the IRS employed the Consumer Price Index (CPI) for inflation measurements. However, following the Tax Cuts and Jobs Act of 2017 (TCJA), it switched to the Chained Consumer Price Index (C-CPI) for adjusting income levels, deductions, and credit values.

These adjustments apply to the tax year 2023, with tax returns to be filed in early 2024. It's important to note that the Tax Foundation, being a 501(c)(3) educational nonprofit, is not equipped to provide personalized tax advice or assistance in tax filing.

For the 2023 tax year, all tax bracket thresholds and filer categories will be indexed for inflation (Table 1). The federal income tax will feature seven rates: 10%, 12%, 22%, 24%, 32%, 35%, and 37%. In 2023, single filers with taxable income exceeding $578,125 and married couples filing jointly with income over $693,750 will be subject to the highest marginal tax rate of 37%.

Table 1. 2023 Federal Income Tax Brackets and Rates for Single Filers, Married Couples Filing Jointly, and Heads of Households

Tax Rate	For Single Filers	For Married Individuals Filing Joint Returns	For Heads of Households
10%	$0 to $11,000	$0 to $22,000	$0 to $15,700
12%	$11,000 to $44,725	$22,000 to $89,450	$15,700 to $59,850
22%	$44,725 to $95,375	$89,450 to $190,750	$59,850 to $95,350
24%	$95,375 to $182,100	$190,750 to $364,200	$95,350 to $182,100
32%	$182,100 to $231,250	$364,200 to $462,500	$182,100 to $231,250
35%	$231,250 to $578,125	$462,500 to $693,750	$231,250 to $578,100
37%	$578,125 or more	$693,750 or more	$578,100 or more

Source: Internal Revenue Service

Standard Deduction and Personal Exemption Adjustments

For the 2023 tax year, the standard deduction is set to rise by $900 for individuals filing alone and $1,800 for those filing jointly, as indicated in Table 2.

The personal exemption will continue to be $0, as the elimination of the personal exemption was a provision of the Tax Cuts and Jobs Act of 2017 (TCJA).

Table 2. 2023 Standard Deduction

Filing Status	Deduction Amount
Single	$13,850
Married Filing Jointly	$27,700
Head of Household	$20,800

Source: Internal Revenue Service

Alternative Minimum Tax Overview

The Alternative Minimum Tax (AMT) was established in the 1960s to ensure that high-income taxpayers could not completely avoid paying individual income taxes. This separate tax system compels high-income taxpayers to calculate their taxes twice: first under the standard income tax system and then under the AMT, paying whichever amount is greater.

AMT uses a different taxable income definition known as Alternative Minimum Taxable Income (AMTI). To shield lower- and middle-income taxpayers from the AMT, a substantial portion of their income can be exempted from AMTI. However, this exemption decreases for higher-income taxpayers. The AMT has two tax rates: 26% and 28%.

For 2023, the exemption amounts are $81,300 for single filers and $126,500 for married couples filing jointly, as shown in Table 3.

Table 3. 2023 Alternative Minimum Tax (AMT) Exemptions

Filing Status	Exemption Amount
Unmarried Individuals	$81,300
Married Filing Jointly	$126,500

Source: Internal Revenue Service

In 2023, any AMTI above $220,700 will be subject to a 28 percent AMT rate for all taxpayers, and $110,350 for those who are married and file separately.

The AMT exemptions begin to reduce at a rate of 25 cents for every dollar of income when AMTI exceeds $578,150 for single filers and $1,156,300 for married couples filing jointly, as noted in Table 4.

Table 4. 2023 Alternative Minimum Tax (AMT) Exemption Phaseout Thresholds

Filing Status	Threshold
Unmarried Individuals	$578,150
Married Filing Jointly	$1,156,300

Source: Internal Revenue Service

2023 Earned Income Tax Credit

In 2023, the highest Earned Income Tax Credit (EITC) available to both single and joint filers without children is $560, as indicated in Table 5. For filers with dependents, the maximum credit increases to $3,995 for one child, $6,604 for two children, and $7,430 for three or more children.

Table 5. 2024 Earned Income Tax Credit (EITC) Parameters

Filing Status		No Children	One Child	2 Children	3 or + Children
Single or Head of Household	Income at Max Credit	$7,840	$11,750	$16,510	$16,510
	Maximum Credit	$600	$3,995	$6,604	$7,430
	Phaseout Begins	$9,800	$21,560	$21,560	$21,560
	Phaseout Ends (Credit Equals Zero)	17,640	46,560	52,918	56,838
Married Filing Jointly	Income at Max Credit	$7,840	$11,750	$16,510	$16,510
	Maximum Credit	$600	$3,995	$6,604	$7,430
	Phaseout Begins	$16,370	$28,120	$28,120	$28,120
	Phaseout Ends (Credit Equals Zero)	24,210	53,120	59,478	63,398

Source: Internal Revenue Service

Child Tax Credit Update

The maximum Child Tax Credit remains at $2,000 per eligible child and does not adjust with inflation. However, the refundable part of the Child Tax Credit, which adjusts for inflation, will rise from $1,500 to $1,600 in 2023.

Capital Gains Tax Rates and Brackets (Long-Term Capital Gains)

Long-term capital gains are subject to different tax brackets and rates compared to ordinary income, as detailed in Table 6.

Table 6. 2023 Capital Gains Tax Brackets

	For Unmarried Individuals, Taxable Income Over	For Married Individuals Filing Joint Returns, Taxable Income Over	For Heads of Households, Taxable Income Over
0%	$0	$0	$0
15%	$44,625	$89,250	$59,750
20%	$492,300	$553,850	$523,050

Source: Internal Revenue Service

Qualified Business Income Deduction (Sec. 199A)

The Tax Cuts and Jobs Act of 2017 (TCJA) provides a 20 percent deduction for pass-through entities. The limits on this deduction start to phase in for taxpayers earning more than $182,100, or $364,200 for those filing jointly, in 2023, as shown in Table 7.

Table 7. 2024 Qualified Business Income Deduction Thresholds

Filing Status	Threshold
Unmarried Individuals	$182,100
Married Filing Jointly	$364,200

Source: Internal Revenue Service

Annual Exclusion for Gifts

In 2023, gifts up to $17,000 per person are tax-exempt, an increase from the previous $16,000 limit. Additionally, the exclusion amount for gifts to non-U.S. citizen spouses has been raised to $175,000 from $164,000.

Answer Sheet

A B C D
A B C D
A B C D
A B C D
A B C D
A B C D
A B C D
A B C D
A B C D
A B C D
A B C D
A B C D
A B C D
A B C D
A B C D
A B C D
A B C D
A B C D
A B C D
A B C D
A B C D
A B C D
A B C D
A B C D
A B C D
A B C D
A B C D
A B C D

A B C D
A B C D
A B C D
A B C D
A B C D
A B C D
A B C D
A B C D
A B C D
A B C D
A B C D
A B C D
A B C D
A B C D
A B C D
A B C D
A B C D
A B C D
A B C D
A B C D
A B C D
A B C D
A B C D
A B C D
A B C D
A B C D
A B C D
A B C D

A B C D
A B C D
A B C D
A B C D
A B C D
A B C D
A B C D
A B C D
A B C D
A B C D
A B C D
A B C D
A B C D
A B C D
A B C D
A B C D
A B C D
A B C D
A B C D
A B C D
A B C D
A B C D
A B C D
A B C D
A B C D
A B C D
A B C D
A B C D

A B C D
A B C D
A B C D
A B C D
A B C D
A B C D
A B C D
A B C D
A B C D
A B C D
A B C D
A B C D
A B C D
A B C D
A B C D
A B C D
A B C D
A B C D
A B C D
A B C D
A B C D
A B C D
A B C D
A B C D
A B C D
A B C D
A B C D
A B C D

Answer Sheet

A	B	C	D	A	B	C	D	A	B	C	D	A	B	C	D
A	B	C	D	A	B	C	D	A	B	C	D	A	B	C	D
A	B	C	D	A	B	C	D	A	B	C	D	A	B	C	D
A	B	C	D	A	B	C	D	A	B	C	D	A	B	C	D
A	B	C	D	A	B	C	D	A	B	C	D	A	B	C	D
A	B	C	D	A	B	C	D	A	B	C	D	A	B	C	D
A	B	C	D	A	B	C	D	A	B	C	D	A	B	C	D
A	B	C	D	A	B	C	D	A	B	C	D	A	B	C	D
A	B	C	D	A	B	C	D	A	B	C	D	A	B	C	D
A	B	C	D	A	B	C	D	A	B	C	D	A	B	C	D
A	B	C	D	A	B	C	D	A	B	C	D	A	B	C	D
A	B	C	D	A	B	C	D	A	B	C	D	A	B	C	D
A	B	C	D	A	B	C	D	A	B	C	D	A	B	C	D
A	B	C	D	A	B	C	D	A	B	C	D	A	B	C	D
A	B	C	D	A	B	C	D	A	B	C	D	A	B	C	D
A	B	C	D	A	B	C	D	A	B	C	D	A	B	C	D
A	B	C	D	A	B	C	D	A	B	C	D	A	B	C	D
A	B	C	D	A	B	C	D	A	B	C	D	A	B	C	D
A	B	C	D	A	B	C	D	A	B	C	D	A	B	C	D
A	B	C	D	A	B	C	D	A	B	C	D	A	B	C	D
A	B	C	D	A	B	C	D	A	B	C	D	A	B	C	D
A	B	C	D	A	B	C	D	A	B	C	D	A	B	C	D
A	B	C	D	A	B	C	D	A	B	C	D	A	B	C	D
A	B	C	D	A	B	C	D	A	B	C	D	A	B	C	D
A	B	C	D	A	B	C	D	A	B	C	D	A	B	C	D
A	B	C	D	A	B	C	D	A	B	C	D	A	B	C	D
A	B	C	D	A	B	C	D	A	B	C	D	A	B	C	D
A	B	C	D	A	B	C	D	A	B	C	D	A	B	C	D

Answer Sheet

A B C D	A B C D	A B C D	A B C D
A B C D	A B C D	A B C D	A B C D
A B C D	A B C D	A B C D	A B C D
A B C D	A B C D	A B C D	A B C D
A B C D	A B C D	A B C D	A B C D
A B C D	A B C D	A B C D	A B C D
A B C D	A B C D	A B C D	A B C D
A B C D	A B C D	A B C D	A B C D
A B C D	A B C D	A B C D	A B C D
A B C D	A B C D	A B C D	A B C D
A B C D	A B C D	A B C D	A B C D
A B C D	A B C D	A B C D	A B C D
A B C D	A B C D	A B C D	A B C D
A B C D	A B C D	A B C D	A B C D
A B C D	A B C D	A B C D	A B C D
A B C D	A B C D	A B C D	A B C D
A B C D	A B C D	A B C D	A B C D
A B C D	A B C D	A B C D	A B C D
A B C D	A B C D	A B C D	A B C D
A B C D	A B C D	A B C D	A B C D
A B C D	A B C D	A B C D	A B C D
A B C D	A B C D	A B C D	A B C D
A B C D	A B C D	A B C D	A B C D
A B C D	A B C D	A B C D	A B C D
A B C D	A B C D	A B C D	A B C D
A B C D	A B C D	A B C D	A B C D
A B C D	A B C D	A B C D	A B C D
A B C D	A B C D	A B C D	A B C D

Answer Sheet

A B C D
A B C D
A B C D
A B C D
A B C D
A B C D
A B C D
A B C D
A B C D
A B C D
A B C D
A B C D
A B C D
A B C D
A B C D
A B C D
A B C D
A B C D
A B C D
A B C D
A B C D
A B C D
A B C D
A B C D
A B C D
A B C D
A B C D
A B C D

A B C D
A B C D
A B C D
A B C D
A B C D
A B C D
A B C D
A B C D
A B C D
A B C D
A B C D
A B C D
A B C D
A B C D
A B C D
A B C D
A B C D
A B C D
A B C D
A B C D
A B C D
A B C D
A B C D
A B C D
A B C D
A B C D
A B C D
A B C D

A B C D
A B C D
A B C D
A B C D
A B C D
A B C D
A B C D
A B C D
A B C D
A B C D
A B C D
A B C D
A B C D
A B C D
A B C D
A B C D
A B C D
A B C D
A B C D
A B C D
A B C D
A B C D
A B C D
A B C D
A B C D
A B C D
A B C D
A B C D

A B C D
A B C D
A B C D
A B C D
A B C D
A B C D
A B C D
A B C D
A B C D
A B C D
A B C D
A B C D
A B C D
A B C D
A B C D
A B C D
A B C D
A B C D
A B C D
A B C D
A B C D
A B C D
A B C D
A B C D
A B C D
A B C D
A B C D
A B C D

Answer Sheet

A B C D	A B C D	A B C D	A B C D
A B C D	A B C D	A B C D	A B C D
A B C D	A B C D	A B C D	A B C D
A B C D	A B C D	A B C D	A B C D
A B C D	A B C D	A B C D	A B C D
A B C D	A B C D	A B C D	A B C D
A B C D	A B C D	A B C D	A B C D
A B C D	A B C D	A B C D	A B C D
A B C D	A B C D	A B C D	A B C D
A B C D	A B C D	A B C D	A B C D
A B C D	A B C D	A B C D	A B C D
A B C D	A B C D	A B C D	A B C D
A B C D	A B C D	A B C D	A B C D
A B C D	A B C D	A B C D	A B C D
A B C D	A B C D	A B C D	A B C D
A B C D	A B C D	A B C D	A B C D
A B C D	A B C D	A B C D	A B C D
A B C D	A B C D	A B C D	A B C D
A B C D	A B C D	A B C D	A B C D
A B C D	A B C D	A B C D	A B C D
A B C D	A B C D	A B C D	A B C D
A B C D	A B C D	A B C D	A B C D
A B C D	A B C D	A B C D	A B C D
A B C D	A B C D	A B C D	A B C D
A B C D	A B C D	A B C D	A B C D
A B C D	A B C D	A B C D	A B C D
A B C D	A B C D	A B C D	A B C D
A B C D	A B C D	A B C D	A B C D

Answer Sheet

A	B	C	D	A	B	C	D	A	B	C	D	A	B	C	D
A	B	C	D	A	B	C	D	A	B	C	D	A	B	C	D
A	B	C	D	A	B	C	D	A	B	C	D	A	B	C	D
A	B	C	D	A	B	C	D	A	B	C	D	A	B	C	D
A	B	C	D	A	B	C	D	A	B	C	D	A	B	C	D
A	B	C	D	A	B	C	D	A	B	C	D	A	B	C	D
A	B	C	D	A	B	C	D	A	B	C	D	A	B	C	D
A	B	C	D	A	B	C	D	A	B	C	D	A	B	C	D
A	B	C	D	A	B	C	D	A	B	C	D	A	B	C	D
A	B	C	D	A	B	C	D	A	B	C	D	A	B	C	D
A	B	C	D	A	B	C	D	A	B	C	D	A	B	C	D
A	B	C	D	A	B	C	D	A	B	C	D	A	B	C	D
A	B	C	D	A	B	C	D	A	B	C	D	A	B	C	D
A	B	C	D	A	B	C	D	A	B	C	D	A	B	C	D
A	B	C	D	A	B	C	D	A	B	C	D	A	B	C	D
A	B	C	D	A	B	C	D	A	B	C	D	A	B	C	D
A	B	C	D	A	B	C	D	A	B	C	D	A	B	C	D
A	B	C	D	A	B	C	D	A	B	C	D	A	B	C	D
A	B	C	D	A	B	C	D	A	B	C	D	A	B	C	D
A	B	C	D	A	B	C	D	A	B	C	D	A	B	C	D
A	B	C	D	A	B	C	D	A	B	C	D	A	B	C	D
A	B	C	D	A	B	C	D	A	B	C	D	A	B	C	D
A	B	C	D	A	B	C	D	A	B	C	D	A	B	C	D
A	B	C	D	A	B	C	D	A	B	C	D	A	B	C	D
A	B	C	D	A	B	C	D	A	B	C	D	A	B	C	D
A	B	C	D	A	B	C	D	A	B	C	D	A	B	C	D
A	B	C	D	A	B	C	D	A	B	C	D	A	B	C	D
A	B	C	D	A	B	C	D	A	B	C	D	A	B	C	D

Answer Sheet

A B C D	A B C D	A B C D	A B C D
A B C D	A B C D	A B C D	A B C D
A B C D	A B C D	A B C D	A B C D
A B C D	A B C D	A B C D	A B C D
A B C D	A B C D	A B C D	A B C D
A B C D	A B C D	A B C D	A B C D
A B C D	A B C D	A B C D	A B C D
A B C D	A B C D	A B C D	A B C D
A B C D	A B C D	A B C D	A B C D
A B C D	A B C D	A B C D	A B C D
A B C D	A B C D	A B C D	A B C D
A B C D	A B C D	A B C D	A B C D
A B C D	A B C D	A B C D	A B C D
A B C D	A B C D	A B C D	A B C D
A B C D	A B C D	A B C D	A B C D
A B C D	A B C D	A B C D	A B C D
A B C D	A B C D	A B C D	A B C D
A B C D	A B C D	A B C D	A B C D
A B C D	A B C D	A B C D	A B C D
A B C D	A B C D	A B C D	A B C D
A B C D	A B C D	A B C D	A B C D
A B C D	A B C D	A B C D	A B C D
A B C D	A B C D	A B C D	A B C D
A B C D	A B C D	A B C D	A B C D
A B C D	A B C D	A B C D	A B C D
A B C D	A B C D	A B C D	A B C D
A B C D	A B C D	A B C D	A B C D
A B C D	A B C D	A B C D	A B C D

ANSWER SHEET

A B C D	A B C D	A B C D	A B C D
A B C D	A B C D	A B C D	A B C D
A B C D	A B C D	A B C D	A B C D
A B C D	A B C D	A B C D	A B C D
A B C D	A B C D	A B C D	A B C D
A B C D	A B C D	A B C D	A B C D
A B C D	A B C D	A B C D	A B C D
A B C D	A B C D	A B C D	A B C D
A B C D	A B C D	A B C D	A B C D
A B C D	A B C D	A B C D	A B C D
A B C D	A B C D	A B C D	A B C D
A B C D	A B C D	A B C D	A B C D
A B C D	A B C D	A B C D	A B C D
A B C D	A B C D	A B C D	A B C D
A B C D	A B C D	A B C D	A B C D
A B C D	A B C D	A B C D	A B C D
A B C D	A B C D	A B C D	A B C D
A B C D	A B C D	A B C D	A B C D
A B C D	A B C D	A B C D	A B C D
A B C D	A B C D	A B C D	A B C D
A B C D	A B C D	A B C D	A B C D
A B C D	A B C D	A B C D	A B C D
A B C D	A B C D	A B C D	A B C D
A B C D	A B C D	A B C D	A B C D
A B C D	A B C D	A B C D	A B C D
A B C D	A B C D	A B C D	A B C D
A B C D	A B C D	A B C D	A B C D
A B C D	A B C D	A B C D	A B C D

ANSWER SHEET

A B C D	A B C D	A B C D	A B C D
A B C D	A B C D	A B C D	A B C D
A B C D	A B C D	A B C D	A B C D
A B C D	A B C D	A B C D	A B C D
A B C D	A B C D	A B C D	A B C D
A B C D	A B C D	A B C D	A B C D
A B C D	A B C D	A B C D	A B C D
A B C D	A B C D	A B C D	A B C D
A B C D	A B C D	A B C D	A B C D
A B C D	A B C D	A B C D	A B C D
A B C D	A B C D	A B C D	A B C D
A B C D	A B C D	A B C D	A B C D
A B C D	A B C D	A B C D	A B C D
A B C D	A B C D	A B C D	A B C D
A B C D	A B C D	A B C D	A B C D
A B C D	A B C D	A B C D	A B C D
A B C D	A B C D	A B C D	A B C D
A B C D	A B C D	A B C D	A B C D
A B C D	A B C D	A B C D	A B C D
A B C D	A B C D	A B C D	A B C D
A B C D	A B C D	A B C D	A B C D
A B C D	A B C D	A B C D	A B C D
A B C D	A B C D	A B C D	A B C D
A B C D	A B C D	A B C D	A B C D
A B C D	A B C D	A B C D	A B C D
A B C D	A B C D	A B C D	A B C D
A B C D	A B C D	A B C D	A B C D
A B C D	A B C D	A B C D	A B C D

Answer Sheet

A B C D	A B C D	A B C D	A B C D
A B C D	A B C D	A B C D	A B C D
A B C D	A B C D	A B C D	A B C D
A B C D	A B C D	A B C D	A B C D
A B C D	A B C D	A B C D	A B C D
A B C D	A B C D	A B C D	A B C D
A B C D	A B C D	A B C D	A B C D
A B C D	A B C D	A B C D	A B C D
A B C D	A B C D	A B C D	A B C D
A B C D	A B C D	A B C D	A B C D
A B C D	A B C D	A B C D	A B C D
A B C D	A B C D	A B C D	A B C D
A B C D	A B C D	A B C D	A B C D
A B C D	A B C D	A B C D	A B C D
A B C D	A B C D	A B C D	A B C D
A B C D	A B C D	A B C D	A B C D
A B C D	A B C D	A B C D	A B C D
A B C D	A B C D	A B C D	A B C D
A B C D	A B C D	A B C D	A B C D
A B C D	A B C D	A B C D	A B C D
A B C D	A B C D	A B C D	A B C D
A B C D	A B C D	A B C D	A B C D
A B C D	A B C D	A B C D	A B C D
A B C D	A B C D	A B C D	A B C D
A B C D	A B C D	A B C D	A B C D
A B C D	A B C D	A B C D	A B C D
A B C D	A B C D	A B C D	A B C D
A B C D	A B C D	A B C D	A B C D

Made in the USA
Las Vegas, NV
01 September 2024